KIMBERLEY

STORIES

EDITED BY
SANDY TOUSSAINT

First published 2012 by
FREMANTLE PRESS
25 Quarry Street, Fremantle 6160
(PO Box 158, North Fremantle 6159)
Western Australia
www.fremantlepress.com.au

Consultant editor Georgia Richter
Cover design Ally Crimp
Printed by Everbest Printing Company, China
Map by Chris Crook, Country Cartographics

National Library of Australia
Cataloguing-in-Publication entry

Kimberley Stories / edited by Sandy Toussaint
1st ed.
9781921888823 (pbk)
Other authors/contributors: Toussaint, Sandy.

A823.4

 Government of **Western Australia**
Department of **Culture and the Arts**

Publication of this title was assisted by the Commonwealth Government
through the Australia Council, its arts funding and advisory body. The
publisher also gratefully acknowledges the assistance of the Kimberley Society.

KIMBERLEY

STORIES

**EDITED BY
SANDY TOUSSAINT**

FREMANTLE
PRESS
fine independent publishing

CONTENTS

Lyrics, poetry, and a play-ful extract

PLACES NAMED IN THE TEXT

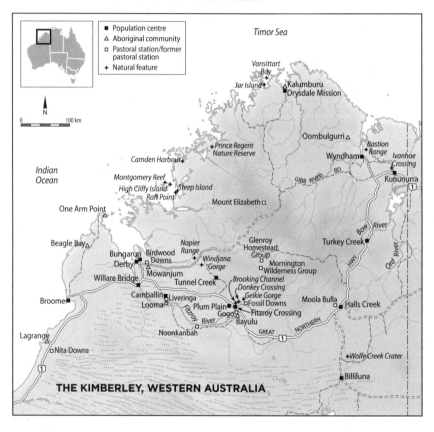

Legend:
- ■ Population centre
- △ Aboriginal community
- □ Pastoral station/former pastoral station
- + Natural feature

0   100 km

N

Timor Sea

Indian Ocean

Vansittart Bay
Jar Island+
Kalumburu△
Drysdale Mission■

Prince Regent Nature Reserve+
Camden Harbour+

Oombulgurri△

Bastion Range+
Wyndham■
Ivanhoe Crossing
Kununurra

GIBB RIVER RD

Montgomery Reef+
High Cliffy Island+
Raft Point+
Steep Island+
Mount Elizabeth□

One Arm Point△

Beagle Bay△

Bungarun
Derby■
Birdwood Downs□
Napier Range+
Windjana Gorge+
Glenroy Homestead Group□
Mornington△
Wilderness Group□
Turkey Creek■

Bow River
HWY
Ord River

Willare Bridge
Mowanjum△
Tunnel Creek+
Brooking Channel
Donkey Crossing
Geikie Gorge+
Fossil Downs□
Moola Bulla□
Halls Creek■

Broome■

Camballin■
Looma△
Liveringa□
Plum Plain□
Gogo□
Bayulu△
Fitzroy Crossing■
Fitzroy River

Lagrange△
Nita Downs□
Noonkanbah□
GREAT NORTHERN HWY

Wolfe Creek Crater+

Bililuna■

THE KIMBERLEY, WESTERN AUSTRALIA

INTRODUCTION
SANDY TOUSSAINT

This book is about the Kimberley as a lived and loved place. It is also about writers and writing, and it is about readers and reading. It was not conceived with a singular view of the Kimberley, or of writers and readers, but with an interest in bringing the diversity of Kimberley life to a wide audience through the words, ideas and emphases of Indigenous and non-Indigenous writers, both established and new. Whilst many contributors identify as authors of literary fiction or as poets, there are others for whom these titles don't easily fit – anthropologists, environmentalists, historians, journalists, and lawyers, who (especially on an occasion like this) also write creatively. Such a literary mix expands our view of what constitutes an author; it also tells us more about the variegated nature of a remote and iconic Australian setting, and the uniqueness of the Kimberley landscape as inspiration. Reader engagement with the texts, and their responses, will also vary, especially when a reader's familiarity with the Kimberley comes into play. Whilst some readers will experience a few 'Ah ha!' or 'Yes ...'

moments, others will find themselves rethinking some of their assumptions. Others will simply enjoy the pleasure of reading insightfully woven narratives and poems, and stories that are well told.

This is not the first work inspired by the Kimberley; others have gone before, others will follow. World Heritage–listed, the red earth and ecology of the Kimberley encompass a vast and rugged region of northern Western Australia, Australia's largest state. The Kimberley is bordered by a significant coastline to the west and north, rangelands and desert to the south-east, and interconnecting rivers and waterholes that support interdependent wildlife. Six regional towns (Broome, Derby, Fitzroy Crossing, Halls Creek, Wyndham and Kununurra), and at least sixty Indigenous communities and outstations, punctuate the landscape. The past and present homeland of Aboriginal groups, and a non-Aboriginal population that has increasingly established homes and families in the region, the Kimberley and its people have already provided a cultural and poetic backdrop for numerous authors. These include, but are by no means limited to, Peter Docker, Robert Drewe, Mary Durack, Ion Idriess, Gail Jones, Steve Kinnane and Tim Winton. The Kimberley has also marked a place for academic writing, as well as the production of anthologies, popular culture magazines, and tourist information. What distinguishes *Kimberley Stories* is its focus on the interconnections between people and place, and a complement of styles that are both Kimberley-born, and Kimberley-inspired.

The Kimberley was put on the literary map by the distinctive work of Aboriginal author, playwright and lyricist, the notable Jimmy Chi. A contributor to this collection, Chi's renowned play (later a film), *Bran Nue Dae*, is both beacon and inspiration in the world of Kimberley writing. Chi's work managed to turn a literary page in a way that not only drew attention to Indigenous writers, but to the Kimberley itself. Publications by a number of Indigenous and non-Indigenous authors (sometimes as collaborators, as with the work of Pat Lowe and Walmajarri artist, Jimmy Pike) have expanded this body of work, and two comparatively small publishing houses, Backroom Press and Magabala Books, are now established in the coastal town of Broome. A Kimberley Writers Festival also occurs once a year in the East Kimberley town of Kununurra.

Indigenous and non-Indigenous authors, both recognised and emerging, invite readers to get to know the Kimberley in moving, creative, troubling and sometimes amusing ways. Through a blend of literary devices that take readers into the region's social, cultural and environmental life, contributors make plain that the Kimberley and storytelling are close cousins.

The Kimberley as a lived-place, and as a place in one's memory or imagination, occupies the work of most contributors. Kate Auty canvasses the view that, once known and experienced, the Kimberley and its people never quite leave one's mind. Others convey, and sometimes opaquely filter, slightly different subject matter, such as in the mesh of texture and colour to signal both life and death, reflection about memories, cultures, and languages, emotional attachment to loved places and interdependent species, and the simple joy of being at home in the Kimberley. Underscoring these broad themes, Lesley Corbett intertwines the love of a river with the love of those most dear to her, and thirteen-year-old Luisa Mitchell makes plain that she would rather have the 'good old Kimberley over Perth any day'. Joyfulness of place is also evident in Marminjiya Joy Nuggett's story about the excitement of fishing for barramundi in the mighty Fitzroy River. Elsewhere the Kimberley is shown as revealing unexpected connections between two seemingly distinct cultures. Donna Bing-Ying Mak writes about the shared etiquette and sociality between life in the Kimberley and China, and Kelvin Garlett shows how storytelling brings two Australian Aboriginal men from entirely different locations together. Steve Hawke ruminates on the distinct meanings embedded in English and the Indigenous Bunuba language during rehearsals for a play about a legendary Bunuba figure, Jandamarra.

Juxtaposition also informs this collection. Via a questioning humour, Peter Bibby's script extract 'From *Escapadia*' invites readers on a road trip that scoops up a day filled by activities, words and silences among six interrelated characters. Bibby's play-ful emphasis is counterbalanced by other authors who evoke a distinct sense of the profundity and vulnerability of people and wildlife in the natural environment, as in Pat Lowe's short story 'Seagull'. A sense of unease beneath everyday life percolates the blend of words and ideas that imbue

Bonita Mason's 'Just leave it. It's good the way it is.', the grainy poetry of Robyn Wells' 'butcherman', and the soulful lyrics of Jimmy Chi in his telling rendition of life in a northern town.

The Kimberley's rich, complex and sometimes hidden history is also a topic of inquiry and reflection. While Kate Auty queries the implications of a White colonial history through the lens of a tree scarred with the number 303, Pat Mamanyjun Torres's trajectory is both past and present. For Torres, Aboriginal history is current, familial, cultural, and country-focused: the intergenerational Kimberley landscape is an ancestral gift to be actively cherished and forever protected. Steve Gome's piece falls within the history oeuvre in a personal way. Gome leads readers back to an event he witnessed as a young child at the Yungngora Community at the Noonkanbah Pastoral Station. With a kangaroo hunt as a focus to explore the child he was and the adult he has become, Gome considers the influence of Indigenous sociality and spirituality on his 'Double vision' reckoning. In a contribution that is also reflective, Cathie Clement skilfully navigates her way through a Sherlockian search for history; a disciplined meandering that eventually hooks her into being a Kimberley historian.

Cherished place as both reality and metaphor combine in the shimmering poetry of C. Ann Hobson, the moody emphasis of Leon Henry, and the delicate, deliberate prose of Stephen Scourfield. In each of these works, readers are encouraged to learn, as well as to listen and to question, cultural and emotional aspects of Kimberley life. A more distinct caution, and a desire to unravel assumptions and contradictions, is found in Jacqueline Wright's 'A seasonal unease'. She evokes the ecological and cultural intricacies of place to stress the danger that resource development poses to seasonal, cyclical natural environments, and people's fragile interrelationships with these. Kim Mahood writes with compelling alacrity about the aesthetic, symbolic and material value of art on the run to comment on the immeasurable qualities of silence, politics and space.

Mahood's emphasis can be contrasted with the qualities of sound and action expressed in other work. Murray Jennings' account in 'Sandy's send-off' is a poignant, quirky tale about preparation for, and activities surrounding, a funeral in the East Kimberley town of Halls Creek. Jennings' characters reflect just some of the characters found in other Kimberley towns and communities. In a different way, Richard Davis's poem carries the audience to a Kimberley pastoral station in which an annual rodeo ride illuminates the rugged sociality of pastoral life. While Kelvin Garlett focuses on a dugong hunt to explain the value of storytelling and the qualities of close, distant and arbitrary kin, Sandy Toussaint and Jane Mulcock draw on the symbolic and material qualities of a leaf to reflect the spirit of friendship across time, place and culture. Andrew Burke's 'By your students you'll be taught' reveals the value of retelling stories in different times and places. Drawing on the lyrics and rhythm of the Wanalirri song, Burke guides readers through a day at a Kimberley community school where words and images free, rather than constrain, young and old in a provocative, revealing and respectful way.

Kimberley Stories shows the richness of people's intrinsic connections to each other, and to place. It explores the intricacies of nature, pockets of social distress and disquiet, and it reflects humour, joy and hopefulness. From every vantage point, these qualities tell us something about the nature of the Kimberley, as well as the lives and realities of those who live in the Kimberley, visit from time to time, or aspire to do so.

A NOTE ON INDIGENOUS SPELLINGS AND USAGE

Indigenous words can be spelt in a variety of shared and/or different ways by Aboriginal and Torres Strait Islander people, and by linguists. Historical documents also reveal a range of spellings. In many cases, spellings have been altered over time; for instance, the former spelling of the language group named Punaba has been revised to Bunuba. Indigenous and non-Indigenous contributors to *Kimberley Stories* refer to a spectrum of Kimberley language groups, and interrelated place-names and species. In accordance with local or revised understandings these sometimes differ from prior or alternate usage. Where appropriate, a capital letter has been used to signify a place name, mythic being or socio-cultural concept.

CONNECTIONS TO KIMBERLEY PLACES, PERSONS AND NATURE

ARRIVING, DEPARTING, AND NEVER QUITE LEAVING
KATE AUTY

Exiting north from the Canning Stock Route just short of the Kimberley's Billiluna Community, you drive through a stand of desert oak. In the late afternoon sunlight the oaks sigh and seem to shiver. Even in midwinter the afternoon heat burns a fair skin: late into the day.

To your left you pass a tree stump out of which is carved a coolamon. Or the carving may be a western emblem, a survey marker. It is a little high, about midline. In the middle of the scar is carved '303'. In the Kimberley 303 can really only mean one thing. Firearm. Why anyone would have carved those numbers there is a mystery to us, and nothing in the map elaborates. Would the numbers be for someone leaving or entering the Canning Stock Route? We have just come off the Yiwarra Kuju, as Indigenous people call it, and along the route we have passed a lot of western death iconography: marble and timber headstones fenced by posts and rails. We know that equalisers occurred. For every white death, there is at least one black. Administered by 303? Seems excessive in the bright light of the day.

The Canning is a stock, and now tourist, route. Even in its heyday, it was a rarely used folly supporting a north-western dream of a cattle empire of vast proportions. Named after a colonial explorer called Canning, the route has been a place of sorrow and death since its western incarnation. Canning chained Aboriginal men and women and forced them to take him to a series of native wells: a young woman was released because she kept soiling herself, a man, the 'Moth', who behaved madly, was also released. Others. A Royal Commission in 1908 found nothing untoward had occurred. Canning 'lost' a man called Tobin on the return journey south, close to a place where there are significant rock art sites, because of the taking of 'portmanteaux' of value to local Aboriginal people. Others, non-Aboriginal and Aboriginal, lost their lives bringing cattle through. If there is a story about Indigenous people dying on the route it is usually regarded as a less important story than the one you can read in the non-Indigenous texts, of Canning the man and his triumph over nature. Up, over and after each successive sand dune as recent travellers we come to appreciate the comings and goings of those unaccustomed to the conditions but you also come to respect the ability of Aboriginal women, men and children to turn this part of the world into a place of subsistence. Before becoming a stock route the regularity of the residual chain of small-scale rock and sandy water holes (or 'native wells' as Canning put it) suggests a pathway fitted for other people's purposes. These are ritual and mundane, real and challenging. And they were made all the more difficult by a group of white men riding people down, chaining them up and depriving them of water.

These reflections are about my last time in the Kimberley. It was not so long ago. Charlie and I came off the stock route and put our clothes in a roadside bin. We put our waste, a plastic ten-litre water container, twelve days' worth of rubbish, in the Halls Creek tip. We stopped at Fitzroy Crossing and ate, not knowing the date or even the time. Whilst we were away important things occurred in the wider world. The Beaconsfield miners in Tasmania came up for air, blinking at the light, hairy-nosed wombat-like. My first time was in the 1950s when I took a long drive from Shepparton, Victoria. I was in the parents' car, John and Jean's, a Citroen D19. The Nullarbor Plain (also known as the Nullarbor Highway) was still dirt and we spent cracker night at the Eucla telegraph station letting off rockets. We still have a photograph of my sister Kelly and me standing in the doorway of the station, sand piled up around our feet, in red velvet dresses made from curtains taken from the windows at Maude Street. The western highway up the coast was also dirt. My brother was there too, so we were three kids in the back of the car, John and Jean in the front, changing drivers when tired. I remember waves of bright parrots, and I remember that driving at night meant we lay in the back seat and watched the trees pass between us, and we watched the stars. Until there were no trees. I have no memory of what I now know to be that long, long treeless stretch of road north to Port Hedland. Perhaps I slept?

We stopped in Broome for breakfast but didn't stay when the bacon and eggs arrived at the cafe table with the egg yolk covered by a huntsman spider. It was all legs and round body cooked into the yolk. In an exercise of undisputed defiance we left without paying. Heavy with disappointment, we turned again to the roadway food stock of dried apricots and puffed wheat.

I also have no memory of the road from Broome east up the Great Northern Highway to Wyndham. We propped in the car at the Ivanhoe Crossing, the river being in flood. When we crossed we stopped to stay for three years at the Ord River research station with its cotton and sugar cane, and with other non-Indigenous people from the south, from Holland, and from the Baltic states. The tin roofs of the technical assistants' quarters, out in the paddock, sent ripples of heat back into the sky, visible, destabilising.

The first house we stayed in at the Kimberley Research Station was nearly opposite the mess hall, over the road from the cook's house and facing the river. Trees included jacaranda and poinsettia. Not Indigenous. You had to walk up to the rim or back from the river to find eucalypts. In wildflower season the plain back from the river was a blanket of colour. After rain this was where we caught the tadpoles. The mess hall was to the west of the makeshift barbeque area where a man called Cruikshank used to air guitar 'El Paso' and other western songs before challenging others to swim the river, which he did at least once. The barbeque area also doubled as the outdoor movie theatre where we could watch films brought up from Perth through a hail of fruit bats stimulated by the light.

The one-room school was one street back from the river, past the round concrete out-of-ground pool. My brother Peter could ride his tricycle across the bottom of the pool without needing to come up for breath. He and I started in the school after Christmas; Kelly was the baby and too young.

We moved to a house down the road from the school, past the technical assistants' quarters and next to some of the other scientists' houses. The Thompsons had a Peugeot and three kids. They also had a Dalmatian dog which seemed to have no personality in the way those dogs do. The mothers helped each other and shared. They ordered the supplies together and mostly laughed when the orders arrived out-of-sorts. One year a massive order of toilet paper arrived – dozens and dozens and dozens of rolls. Another time a laminex table arrived with unmatched chairs – a looming, disappointing drama, sorted by sharing.

The Aboriginal kids came over to school from the Ivanhoe Station. They could swim and run and jump better than we ever would. When we marched onto the Fitzroy Crossing oval for school sports and won nothing, Jean said in her wry way, 'You marched on so well, looking wonderful.' We probably did, with the pride kids have about those sort of straight-up things before they realise it is mostly all bullshit.

The teachers took a longer journey than us, literally and figuratively, to get to the Kimberley Research Station School. Young and know-nothing they came up from Perth and, tour of duty done, returned again. It seemed to occur on an annual basis. One nice young woman who lived next door used to make iced coffee after school if we went for a visit. She didn't seem to stay as long as others. One played the melodica, a foolish instrument, but portable. One put silly work puzzles on the blackboard that the Aboriginal kids had no chance of solving – doubled-up words, bad spelling errors. In a cruel twist you had to get the puzzle before you could leave the room for lunch. The teachers always seemed hot, and often flustered. Sometimes an examiner arrived and then there were two teachers in the room. We wrote on slates. I was told, 'Kathryn I don't usually hit girls but I will make an exception for you.' I had been talking and giggling with Carol Gerrard in class. I thought Carol was wonderful. She was calm and poised and didn't seem to care about being chastised, whereas I did. In the schoolyard I seem to remember we mixed, but not well. I remember a white girl arriving who assumed control of games and associations and who invited me to her house in Kununurra for a birthday party which didn't take place. It wasn't even her birthday. The twenty-four mile round trip for my parents, a tense overnight stay and less friendly relations afterwards, is something I remember still. I also remember the Ivanhoe kids and the song 'You are my sunshine'. Years later Yorta Yorta people, Rochelle

Patten and Sandra Bailey, and I, sang it at a campfire at Cummeragunja by the Murray River in Victoria.

We were naughty and swore. When we returned south I knew more swearwords than any other kid in any class I entered. I learned them off one of the white girls. We played mothers and fathers down by the river, captured and lost the butterflies that somehow got through the chicken wire we used as their cage. In the absence of initiative-crushing parental supervision we put our legs in the water to tempt the salties that we knew to be there. We knew because we had seen one great long crocodile carcass laid out under the mess when someone shot it down by the pump station. We knew this too as Jean had a photo, taken over the width of the river, of a great large log-like thing which suddenly, surprisingly, slid into the water, graceful and racy.

That long journey to the Kimberley for one teacher ended as suddenly as it started. You remember these things in segments, as you see things that way when you are shamed enough to wish you could look away. You turn your head but are drawn back in. He arrived, like the others, without any serious notice being taken of the loss of the one who went before. He came to the school in the morning, being there before we arrived. He taught us 'see Betty run' and 'watch Spot jump' stories, and reading skills that, for the white kids, probably had meaning. I have no idea how long he was there before the unwatchable occurred. One of the young Aboriginal girls, fearful of asking to go to the toilet, wet her pants. The teacher was enraged. He forced her nose into her pee. I think we all went home shortly afterwards. We told Jean. Jean told John. Other children may have done the same. I recall John and one of the other scientists getting into the Citroen, going to the teacher's house and driving him to Wyndham airport where he was told to wait for the next plane. For us, the children of the scientists, it was a clear illustration of what was good and bad, what was acceptable and what wasn't. For us nevertheless the weeks that followed were wonderful. Jean taught us 'A for apple' and 'B for bat' at home, with marvellous flexible school hours.

Then another teacher came and we all went back to school. We in the scientists' camp were clear about what had happened but I don't know whether the Aboriginal kids were. That was the way it was. Even when something proper or good happened we struggled with the means to convey the message. As children we were probably better at passing the message on than the adults but we weren't good at explaining stuff that happened yesterday.

Years later I think that this day might have passed unremarkably if it hadn't happened on the Kimberley Research Station, a scientific enclave, where some things were not tolerated. People from the south ... us, not great champions and always going to move on, we nevertheless made a difference, however insignificant in the great scheme of things, on that day.

When it came time to leave, the Whites in recently created Kununurra were still trying to segregate the newly opened school. Again scientists and the pedal radio threat of exposure stopped them. The school opened to all. But the Kununurra Club remained segregated for years before the hotelier Karmapesci chained a member of the Green family and his mate to the bumper bar of his car and dusted them with flour overnight. The litigation over that conduct was the first time an Aboriginal person sued for damages and won. Others, outsiders, drove that case.

The Kimberley was a place where I grew out, not even knowing it was happening. Days like that day in the classroom have been formative for me. All of my Kimberley arrivals since have been followed by a departure, but the place leaves its impact and you never quite leave. Things happen in the Kimberley that don't happen in other places. The history is still, almost, and it is contemporary and raw. It is a place where a blend of people from elsewhere can and still does make a difference.

But so much will always remain unexplained and unexplored, like the number 303 carved into the stump of a Kimberley tree.

A SEASONAL UNEASE
JACQUELINE WRIGHT

When I was a little girl, my father took me outside. Crouching down, he put his arm around me. I could smell the Brylcream in his hair. My hip nestled easily into the crease of his elbow.

'What colour is the grass?' he asked.

'Green,' I answered with five-year-old affirmity.

He nodded.

Later that night, he took me outside again.

'What colour is the grass?' he asked.

I peered into the darkness. 'Black?' I frowned. 'Grey?'

This, I remembered when I moved to the tropics. Woken by the croaking of green tree frogs, I lay in bed watching as the blackness morphed into a shades-of-grey world then sprouted with astounding light: earthen, green and watery. It reminded me how little I had seen of the Kimberley, despite the fact that I had travelled it extensively through previous work.

My understanding of country was shaped by European disposition. The four seasons ran in my blood. My parents, you see, were English and had an intimate association with them. Mum grew up tramping the fields and hedgerows of England and Europe. With her college girlfriends, she hiked from one village to the next, along paths lined with herbs, crocus and cyclamen. As a child, she gathered wild strawberries and windfall apples, picked snowdrops. Mum spoke of pea-soup fogs, tobogganing, meadows of buttercups, the multi-layered colouring of trees. Greenness like I'd never seen.

But it was black mud, patchwork reconstruction and entrenched attitudes of the coal mines that eventually carried my father away into a career powered by the pristine water of the Snowy River. I was born in the river town of Corryong and spent the first years of my life growing up in the construction town of Bella Vista. There is a picture postcard of it, tucked away in the pages of a photograph album. Splash of colour in amongst the black and white photographs with scalloped edges. Small town digging into the slope of a mountain topped with snow. Blue sky carefully painted in around the clouds. It looks just like a European village, shaped by centuries, instead of one put together and pulled down just as easily as a child's Lego set. My father reminisces about fishing for trout in the freezing tributaries upstream from the hydro-electricity turbines. He talks of snow and plenty of it. Twenty-eight feet drifts. Snow piled up to the telegraph wires. So deep you could walk from the roof of one house to the next. And old Mr Gordon, poor fellow, froze to death, not ten metres from someone's front door step. Slipped on the ice and broke his ankle. No one heard his cries. Snow's like that; it muffles sound.

I tobogganed at Bella Vista, in a plastic baby bath, down the slope of the back garden well, fielded by Dad at the bottom. Then his work took us further north and inland. Away from winters to a country of red-dirt roads, mosquitoes and heat that wore my mother down. When we moved to Tasmania, it was a blessing, she always said. The seasons separated in Hobart. Geraniums flourished and, sometimes, there was snow. Mum dressed her daughters in wellington boots and mittens. She buttoned our coats and took us to the park so we could scuff around in the autumn leaves. Then we moved, again, permanently this time, to another city, where she could experience all her English seasons in one day.

Despite our huge national efforts to cling to them, the four seasons are blurred around the edges in many parts of Australia. Summer and winter whittle away at autumn and spring. The seasons are marked by droughts and dust storms; raging bushfires and floods. And those poor cousins ... autumn and spring ... we see less and less of them the further north we travel. In the tropics there are two seasons – the Wet and the Dry.

When I first moved to the satellite community of 12 Mile, just outside of Broome, I struggled with the Wet and the Dry. Tried wrestling them into the categories 'summer' and 'winter' respectively. I recall announcing this to the honey man as he tossed pancakes at the Saturday markets behind a palisade of golden jars. 'Well I dunno 'bout that.' He drizzled his Best Desert Blend over a stack of three. 'If you describe winter as six months of sparkling weather in the high twenties with only a squeeze of rain, I spose winter's the word for you.'

The Yawuru people of Broome recognise six seasons. Their seasons signal matching and hatching. Sleeping, waking, moving. The cooking up and the dishing out of storms. Different kinds of rain throughout the year: the showers from washed out winter skies; downpours flicked out from the tail of a cyclone; the knock 'em down rain which takes you by surprise at the end of the Wet; the drip, drip of sea fogs chased back into the ocean by the desert easterlies. Those kinds of seasons. But school children in the tropics still stick cotton wool snowballs onto paper pine trees while local businesses stick up print-outs from the Bureau of Meteorology showing spiralling circles of tropical lows. The children paste pictures of autumn leaves around the classroom while countrymen up on the peninsula keep an eye out for grazing dugong.

My sense of the seasonal blinkered me. It turned me into a grass is always greener type of girl and drove me to hack away at native bush, plant lawn and palms, while all around the wet season sprouted greenness like I'd never seen. It took a great many more years of tropical living to give up on wrestling this country into preconceived packages. I have been living here for thirteen years, yet still the six seasons continue to elude me. I can distinguish only three, no matter how hard I try.

1. The Wet – build-up time

Greetings from Broome! The local radio station announces: 'Scattered showers in the Kimberley.' This means it could rain somewhere in an area the size of Northern Europe. It's hot, beer-drinking, shorts and thongs type weather. Clouds heap themselves into something atomic. Electrical storms light up the night sky. Grumble of thunder. Rain sticking its tongue out some place I'm not. Visitors thin out and parking spots are abundant. Days of queuing are over. Local residents catch up on gossip after their long hibernation during the tourist season. We're all waiting, just waiting for rain but it's like waiting for a meteorite to take out the earth.

2. The Wet – rainy time

Rain finally arrives. Deliver us from humidity! Fire and brimstone storms. Cyclones expected, but they are truly whimsical creatures who pick up the skirts of their tropical low furies and cross the coast wherever they please. Smell of wet earth and tarmac. Slap of frog flesh against concrete. Plump geckos, flying ants, lavender beetles. Gardens flap with bird life. Flowering and fruiting. The only place to eat a mango is in a bath.

3. The Dry
The dry is a medal for those who have sat through the Wet. A constellation, known as the 'Seven Sisters' here and 'The Pleiades' elsewhere, signals its beginning. Dragonflies on the wind and lines of caravans down the highway. The queue at the post office snakes out of the door and down the street. Native foliage changes from green to silver-grey. Sudden storms flatten the grasses. Dryness and flowering wattle. Easterly winds barrel in from the desert. Hay fever sneezes. The ocean is as fresh as peppermint. Nights cold enough for fires.

This is the picture-postcard view. A splash amongst the troughs and peaks of national stories, and fantasies involving the remote tropics and pearling towns. Then, there is the experience of year-by-year-by-year living. I've been working hard, harnessing and honing my senses, imagining terrain beyond my preconceptions. But it's small steps and big lessons and, after thirteen years, I'm only just beginning to understand.

It's November, midday to be exact, close-knit heat. The kind that has me leaping off the vinyl seat of a parked car, less a layer of skin. The ground sears the soles of my feet as I wander out to the washing line. Tomatoes roast on their vines. The snappy gums and bloodwoods shed bark and bleed sap. The paucity of bushland allows rare glimpses into our neighbour's block; I see Amelia hanging out the washing in her undies, Sebastian burying a rooster. Agile wallabies limp closer to the house nibbling through reticulation pipes to sip liquid close to boiling point.

A willy-willy dances in from the east whipping up the long-spent ashes of the dry season fire pit. It pulls the scrub into a frenzy dragging foliage into its heart and spitting it out into the roaring blue of the sky. It leaves behind an almost imperceptible sea breeze which will strengthen by the afternoon. I fill up the toddler's pool, but not for the toddler. Instead, I lie in the tepid water, spreading myself out as thin as my body will allow whilst sucking flesh from a mango seed. I imagine myself as some kind of filter, heat trickling through me and out the other side. At night, the toddler tosses himself around the bed and out of his pyjamas.

By December the clouds are spending whole days constructing themselves into fluffy promises. Electrical storms light up Roebuck Bay and the plains beyond. It doesn't take much to set the frogs off – rumble of thunder, slam of a screen door, tap of a hammer or the squwark, squwark, squwarking of blue-winged kookaburras, to get them going. They're so loud I can barely hear myself talking.

'What's that I can hear in the background?' the

Telstra operator asks me.

'It's a chorus of frogs!' I shout and she thinks I'm joking.

But I enjoy them while I can because their performances are numbered, I just know. Cane toads are over the Northern Territory border and advancing fast.

The sea is as warm as bath water but it's safer to swim at the local pool. Once we braved the box jellyfish, the crocodiles and sharks by swimming in packs, fully clothed and armed with a bottle of vinegar, but the irukandji have scared us off for good. These jellyfish are only the size of jellybeans, but the pain has people begging nursing staff to put them out of their misery.

In the supermarket, mince pies and brandy custard, candy canes and baubles are infiltrating the shelves. Cherries are selling at twenty dollars a kilo. I surreptitiously pop one into my mouth wondering what part of the country, or even what country, they come from.

The only visitors we get now are cyclones. They can come from as far away as Queensland. Ingrid did, forming and transforming from cyclone to low pressure system and back again. I think they renamed her twice before she made it to Broome. She crossed state boundaries and switched genders, sank a pearling fleet and flattened an eco-friendly resort. Vance travelled as far south as Exmouth before crossing the coast. Then he trekked through the Goldfields and out into the Great Australian Bight, sweeping what was left of the wheatbelt topsoil out to sea. Ingrid and Vance have proved to me that cyclones, unlike cherries, are never predictable.

'Everyone's as happy as a fox in a chicken coop,' my neighbour says, when it finally does rain. Now we're smack bang in the middle of the Wet, facing another five months of high temperatures, high humidity. Tempers flare. It's the time of year when the Kimberley Mental Health Unit is at its busiest. This is a taste of the kind of behaviour you can expect: digging a two-foot trench across your neighbour's driveway. Or standing dripping wet in your speedos in the shopping centre demanding a refund on leaking goggles. Then there was the year that my friend started knitting ribbed uteruses, in two-tone pink wool.

Out at the washing line, I do the mad slapping march-fly dance, except it isn't March. Shallow-rooted pindan wattles dislodge themselves from the saturated earth and do a slow freefall over cars and driveways. Hakea flowers drip with honeyeaters. The sweet-sick smell of paperbarks clogs the air. Hibiscus, ti-tree, snowball bush, conkerberry, eucalypt, gubinge and magabala flower and fruit. It draws the flying foxes in from the mangroves. Squadrons of them fill the sky in their search and destroy missions. They beat their great leathery wings in the branches and fill the dusk with demonic screeching.

April. Let's not go there. Suffice to say that this is the month that encompasses all of the above except that the atmosphere is cocked and loaded with something like ninety-nine percent humidity. Even the Yawuru call it 'rubbish time'. Clouds of mozzies carry all manner of scary diseases, without a breath of wind to shoo them away. Leather boots go furry with mould and cigarette papers stick together like a string of paper dolls. The washing stays hanging on the line for days. My friend says this is the season when cars break down and men are arseholes.

I should be weeding, mulching and digging the vegie patch. Yet there's little to motivate movement that extends beyond negotiating my way from the air-conditioned house to the air-conditioned car. Mango Pete pauses in his pruning to tell me it's the time of year his scungy date rash cranks up, but, like April, let's not go there. Let's move on to the Dry and it's about time ...

With a smell I can tell, it's beginning. Dragonflies replace the bats and those Seven Sisters are back up in the night sky again, Scorpion rising in the east. A full moon throws its staircase light across an outgoing tide. If I'm lucky, I will spot a salmon sky at sunrise. These skies, the Yawuru seasonal chart tells me, signal the time that I can catch salmon, but I've been confused about this for many years. You see, the flesh of the salmon up here isn't pink, so why's it called a 'salmon sky'? Lucy Malcolm sets me straight, explaining that the clouds resemble the scales of the fish. So it's the texture of the sky, not the colour that tells me salmon have arrived in Roebuck Bay.

'And that cold south-east wind,' she adds. 'Then you

know that bluenose one start running.'

'Running where?' I ask.

'Onto my fishing line!' she smiles and rubs her belly. 'Pangarnu.'

'Pan ... ?'

'We call 'im pangarnu, bluenose salmon,' she says smiling. 'PARN-GARN-U.' She tries the kindergarten approach and by the time I manage to wrap my tongue around the unfamiliar sounds of her language, Lucy has stopped smiling and is laughing.

The mornings are as cold as a mother-in-law's kiss. I move my chair from the shade of the frangipani, so that the equinox sun can wrap me in its cottony warmth. I watch the owl-faced finches construct nests among the prickly pandanus. A bowerbird frets around on the ping-pong table. Its nest is tucked away beneath the conkerberry bushes in a little-traversed corner of the block. The avenue between its dense twig walls is carpeted with pebbles, tek screws, shells and bottle-tops. Silver, white and neutral colours cover the floor inside, while ripe cumquats, green glass and Ming-blue marbles spill out from the front and rear entrances.

The spear-grass is taller than an adult. Easterlies roar in from the desert sucking the green out of plant life and making everything powder dry. When the easterlies get going, I can peg out a load of washing, and by the time I've hung out the last shirt, I can start unpegging the pair of undies I hung up minutes ago. While winter takes a hold in the south and east, we clear firebreaks.

There are a lot of different kinds of fire this time of year: bushfires and burning-off fires, mustering ones, 'fire control programs' lit by Indigenous and non-Indigenous people. I can't discern the line between 'wild' and 'controlled', especially when those easterlies blow and my nostrils seek out which bit of the sky is filled with billowing smoke. One evening a fire jumped the highway and tore through the bush along our street. An easterly fanned the flames until there was a wall of crackling, spitting flame. Grasshoppers pinged into the air and lizards ran helter-skelter to safety. The orange flames raged against a moonless night.

At twilight, the land undergoes a rapid transformation from saturated colour to velvety glow. The setting sun draws the shadows out and drains colour from the sky. Unmuffled by humidity, we hear the road trains thundering down the highway a kilometre or so before they pass our street. We can hear every word our neighbours say as they drink red wine on the verandah while their children fight about whose turn it is to do what. On a full moon, the singing of the butcher birds cuts through the chill air: three high, clear notes, calling and answering, answering and calling. I dredge the depths of my cupboards for that old windcheater and a footie beanie, a scarf even, and warm my hands by the fire. The best wood for cooking is snappy gum. It burns down to leave decent coals into which we bury pangarnu, garden-sweet corn, kumara. We stir-fry vegetables in an old wok with a can of smoked mussels. Eat stews and damper with a tough, golden crust. Sometimes, there are marshmallows on sticks, sparklers, hot chocolate, singing and story after story.

In my home amongst the pindan wattle, I notice more every year. I can see that the grass can be orange, yellow and silver-white. It can grow taller than adults, smell like coconut suntan oil, get knocked down by storms and provide scaffolding to spider webs that are revealed in the foggy mornings. It sprouts and feathers and produces seeds that infiltrate socks and dogs' ears. I notice more, but I do not notice; the temperatures steadily increasing, the sea levels rising or the watertable lowering. But I hear that we're pumping out too much carbon, drawing too much water, salting the land, digging up the country left, right and centre. There's a gas hub planned for north of Broome, that smelter down at Port. Those coal mines and cotton plantations are sucking the rivers dry and that pulp mill is pouring chemicals into the ocean. And what's that thing they're doing on the reef, by the side of the mountain or under that island? You must have heard about it too? Along with the earthquakes, fire-storms, floods, the hailstorms trashing our cars and the mini tornados ripping off our roofs. I've tried to identify how human impact has affected the country up here. I think perhaps there are more mozzies this year, less pangarnu in the bay, later rain, an incursion of irukandji, and a shorter mango season, but my friend the weatherman tells me this anecdotal stuff cannot always be trusted.

I mean to ask Lucy, have the irukandji always been

here? What is different? What is the same? Lucy has lived in this country all of her life, she has been a part of and witness to a great many changes and I want to know if environmental change is among them, but I'm always asking her questions, too many questions. And here's the thing. It takes a very, very long time to understand particular country; much longer than it takes for a person to love it, or own it or ruin it. And a human life must be just a sliver in this time. I find it difficult to imagine nothing but sand and wind, deserts devouring cities, the Gold Coast swallowed up by the ocean, highways that can no longer be used. As water pumps from our bore, out of reticulation pipes and onto the garden and the fruit trees I have planted, I cannot imagine it being as precious as gold, patrolled by men with guns, warred over.

We pack this not-seeing, not-believing world away, drive it deep into the back of our minds and lie to ourselves, lie down and roll over. Drawing the sheet over our faces, closing eyes, we sleep, just sleep, while temperatures soar, weather patterns become more erratic, icecaps break apart and species after species slips away.

ART ON THE RUN
KIM MAHOOD

These days I make art on the run, under pressure, as a
reflex to the itinerant life I lead between Canberra and the
Kimberley. It comes directly out of the projects I work on
with the Aboriginal people of the south-east Kimberley.
Part of this process involves being in the thick of it, which
has its moments of epiphany but is also a test of physical
and psychological resilience. You can't think or write your
way through it, you live it and you use whatever resources
you have to make sense of it.

Sometimes, when the eye and the mind are in accord, and there's a quiet space that lasts long enough to record that moment of clarity, you come up with something that encapsulates the place you are in and the truths it holds.

In the space between two ways of seeing, the risk is that you see nothing clearly.

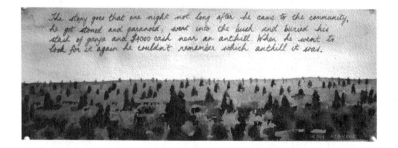

Stories, overheard fragments of conversations, something glimpsed through the window of a vehicle, can say more than all your attempts to put together a coherent narrative.

I've been reduced to the simplest and most portable forms, pencil and watercolour and gouache, making work the size of postcards that are distilled reflections of daily life. They are predominantly landscapes, but text infiltrates them, gnomic fragments that infer the presence of the people I don't paint.

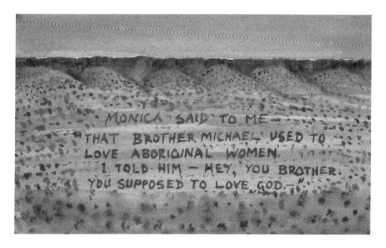

The painting is a means of processing the contradictory forms of perception that are a part of daily life. I work in the slippage between ways of reading country – the art I make is part of a dialogue the language of which is only half-understood by those of us who participate in it. For the moment I accept that this is the best I can do. I would like to spend more time making the work, but it may be that if I had more time I would have less to say.

'JUST LEAVE IT. IT'S GOOD THE WAY IT IS.'
BONITA MASON

Prologue ...

I make a three-day road journey north to Broome, where a new job waits at the Kimberley Land Council. Here, the weather changes overnight from the Wet – hot, humidity and everyday rain – to the Dry. No rain or humidity, it's cooler, the wind comes from the east and the dragonflies swarm. Overnight dew is heavy and some mornings I wake to a warm, thick mist – a shrouded world. In the few weeks I've been here, I know of two people who have died by hanging. One young man and a girl aged nine. A grandmother who is known for her laughter accidentally backs her car over her grandchild. She was raising that child and we have to wait a long time for that grandmother's laughter to return.

I encounter this with an immediacy and completeness I could not have imagined. Whether about international human rights principles, a negotiation over a local mine agreement, or the accidental death of someone's grandchild, these things do not become abstract. They keep their flesh and blood, and their flesh and blood lives down the street and across the road.

They, them, we, us ...

I move to a neighbourhood through which groups of people of all ages walk at the pace of the smallest child. The houses, 1980s-built fibro and brick veneer – some damaged, most cared for – sit on quarter-acre blocks. They were built with no apparent concern for the comfort of their occupants: a series of enclosed rooms, small windows, few gestures towards the cooling breezes. The fibro houses are painted different colours: blues, yellows and ochres, rust and pindan, greens and, one, purple. My neighbour, M___, wears her commitment to the Fremantle Dockers AFL team on her walls. This neighbourhood is known locally as the Bronx.

There are at least three neighbourhoods in Australia that have been known as the Bronx. An East Fairfield social housing estate in south-western Sydney was nicknamed the Bronx in the 1990s, by the Sydney tabloid press but not by its occupants, because of persistent neighbourhood violence. Those areas known as the Bronx in the Western Australian towns of Broome and Carnarvon, both areas where Aboriginal people live (but less exclusively so in Broome), are known as the Bronx by the people who live there, by the people for whom it is home. In all cases, the nickname brings the stigma of poverty, drinking, drug dealing and violence, which denies these places their complexity and life.

M——, my neighbour, knows everyone in the street, except for the white man who lives on the other side of us. But she knows of him – some of what he does, where and with whom. He has the highest fence and front gates in the street, which he keeps locked. He is a drug dealer, known to the police. The days of people coming and going to buy have passed, but he comes and goes quite a bit himself, slamming the gates each time. He has telephone conversations in which he tells the person on the other end of the phone: 'I'm going to fuck you up.' He often screams these things and we can hear every word. We hear his sudden 5 a.m. music so loud it seems to be not only in our rooms, but in our heads. We seek advice from the police. 'Don't talk to him,' they say. 'He once spent time in jail for smashing a glass in someone's face.'

I go to Town Beach to clear my head. It is early stinger season, but the beach at high tide looks and feels irresistible. I enter the water and am carried away on a tide of children. 'Take me deep, take me deep,' the older ones entreat, their arms feeling their way around my neck and shoulders, gently, persistently tugging towards depth. The small children, whom the older children cannot leave without their parents or someone like me to keep an eye on them, hang off older arms or bounce in the shallows. I am theirs and, one at a time, I will take them into the deeper water and bring them back. I will never forget it. I wonder if any of these children live in my neighbourhood.

Our neighbourhood is home to Aboriginal families,

some buying their houses, others renting from Homes-west, and some non-Aboriginal people, many of them single, who have taught and worked alongside Aboriginal people.

It is school holiday time, and visitors and relatives from other communities arrive in the Bronx. Many carouse, the neighbourhood is noisy, and sleep harder to come by. Much of the noise is sociable – loud conversation, laughter, music, singing – some of it at unsociable hours. Some turns from one kind of noise to another. A mob gathers in a front yard a few houses away to talk, play cards, drink, listen to music, party. Late into the night the noise abates. I wake in the early morning dark to one voice rising above the others, an old man who sings:

Old MacDonald had a farm, EE-I-EE-I-O
And on that farm he had some ducks, EE-I-EE-I-O
With a quack, quack here and a quack, quack there ...

The old man sings on, with the odd variation in animals, until after dawn. He becomes angry, drunk-sounding – child's song as threat.

The baby who lives across the road cries and cries. This baby lives in the same house as the 2 a.m. fighting, of the young couple, both late teens, with two small children. The oldest is about eighteen months, the youngest a few weeks at most. The young woman yells: 'I want my smokes, you fucking slut.' Curses ring out: Him: 'My cock not good enough for your cunt. Slut.' Her: 'You fuck off. You think I want your wrinkle, dinkle dick? Fuck off.'

I am amazed at the invention in these and other curses. In the weeks that follow I learn that curses like slut, cunt, prick apply equally to anyone. They are not gender specific. I think about this as I lie in wait for the sound of the fight to change from merely loud, abusive and damaging to violent, crippling, final.

When to call the police? Is it all right to call them when my peace is disturbed, or do I wait until someone's life or safety seems threatened? This choice means listening and waiting for the moment when revelling turns from dangerous to murderous.

'I hate you, you big fat prick,' screamed through the quiet hours before dawn. More screaming, crying and the sound of things smashing. A pause. More incoherent screaming once the light of morning sets in and the day is already too warm. She throws rocks at the house and leaves holes in the recently painted fibro walls. 'Give me my gunja. Give me my gunja. You give me my gunja. Give me my ...' Her voice becomes hoarser, but no less powerful. We call the police. The young man sits quietly on a grey milk crate under the carport, small child in his arms. As we leave for breakfast and peace at Town Beach, he picks up rubbish in the driveway.

A true story (fiction) . . .

As X__ lies in bed, waiting and hoping that the noise will stop, she marvels at the strength and clarity of the young mother's voice. 'With that projection, she should be on the stage,' she thinks. 'Someone ought to tell her. I wonder if I could, and if it would help – help all of us?'

In the daytime she finds herself watching this family. Looking for its different characters, charting its relationships – the young, young parents of a toddler and a baby, the old man who is possibly these child-parents' great-grandfather. She reminds herself of a nosey stereotype, watching through lace curtains. But she feels implicated. From worry and sleep deprivation to, if she doesn't call the police, someone could die. If she does, someone could die.

The next morning X__ sees her neighbour in her front yard. Her neighbour gestures to her to come to the fence, all the time keeping her eyes cast down. 'You shouldn't have got the police last night,' she says. 'We see too much of those cunts as it is.'

'I'm sorry, but too bad,' X__ says. 'Last time I didn't call the police a woman died. Stabbed.'

An old woman walks slowly along the early morning street. She stops and waits for her old dog to catch up, then continues as the sun climbs the sky. Dogs' balls, everywhere. Here, male dogs still have their testicles and dogs live more independent lives than urban dogs in other places; many of them roam in groups.

One warm evening, I walk down the street to visit someone who lives a ten-minute walk away. The street hums with children, dogs, groups of people sitting, talking, playing guitars with missing strings. One man, sitting on a milk crate in his carport, calls out a warning: 'You shouldn't be walking around here at night.' 'But I live here,' I reply. 'That's all right then,' comes back. I walk on, feeling sanctioned.

Journal entry, 27 December, 7.50 a.m.

The street is quiet this morning. On Christmas Eve it knock, knock, knocked on heaven's door from quite early in the morning to quite late the next day. Watch out for the broken glass. It's a feature, a constant, tyre-crunching, glinting part of life. The cardboard formerly containing slabs of beer cans, the cans themselves – twinkling in the hot sun like wrecking jewels.

'You and my own father, what you want to bash me for.' A cry of pain comes across the neighbourhood. 'Why? Why?' These cries go on and on. The words can't be made out, but the sound carries. She'll get a bashing for sure. That's too much pain to sit quietly by. Knock it senseless. Put lumps on her face that don't go away, knock out her teeth, break her arm on a lump of wood, but don't listen to that. It can't be borne.

I can't remember if I call the police or not.

Journal entry, 15 January, 8 a.m

Yesterday evening it rained, just a little. Finally, the weather of the Wet. The cool gusting air before rain brings relief from relentless heat. The brilliance of after-sun brightness, golden light bouncing off and diffuse in the many forms and layers of cloud. Technicolour sky in muted tones, like stepping outside into a brightly lit room.

Journal entry, 15 January, 10 p.m.

It's raining. A storm: close-up lightning and far-off, rumbling on-and-on thunder. It sounds as though we live in a swamp. Swarms of insects, first one kind – flying ants – then another – stink beetles. Frog and geckos call, mostly frogs – different notes of waterborne celebration. Except for the house down the street, where the shouting and the odd scream carries on through the storm. People stand in the rain, seemingly not noticing, while a light so white it is blue lights their night-time street. Anger, grief and misery are a captivating force.

My neighbour, M___, has spare fish from a fishing trip. She offers us some, which we swap for vegetables from our garden. We see small children walking and riding their too-big bikes to school. My neighbour points out the owl in the tree.

Journal entry, 24 April, 7.40 a.m.

Two young men sit drinking across the road. They are talking and laughing, a pram in front of them. The father of the two looks often towards the child in the pram. They seem to be talking about this child as heads and bodies incline towards the pram. Tender.

In the background and getting louder is the tinny tune of the ice-cream van. 'Greensleeves'. The neighbourhood Pied Piper. In the background the young woman yells: 'Who took my gunja? Give me back my gunja.' All is quiet for a while, then: 'Those cunts, they poop their holes, they arseholes.'

The young woman walks past in a red t-shirt, head down, like she's thinking. They reconcile, and keep hurting each other.

They, them, we, us ...

> *WA neighbours are at war as the trend towards higher density housing means residents are living closer than ever before, with one of Perth's major councils reporting about 20,000 neighbourhood complaints every year.*
> *West Australian* newspaper, October 2010

Most of these complaints are about noise – music and loud parties, dogs, air-conditioners. The *West* reports that these complaints and other problems are increasing because of increased density.

> *Broome's residential codings range from R10 to R50. The great majority of new lots that have been created are between 600 sq.m and 900 sq.m. 'Larger' blocks (i.e., greater than 700 sq.m) are justified by climatic factors and the need to allow cooling breezes to*

circulate freely through and between dwellings, and the high ownership levels of larger vehicles (4WDs), boats and caravans, which need to be accommodated on-site.
Broome Shire Council Local Housing Strategy, February 2009

The Broome shire plans to rezone the neighbourhood to R30, which means three houses where now there is one (one house per three hundred square metres). People will be living closer together. Those who live in the area can see the problems. Some of their submissions to council on the proposal say:

The rezoning to higher density will affect the lives of all residents in the area and increase noise, traffic and social problems.

While the area has improved, as most people are willing to get to know their neighbours, the area is socially fragile and the problems need to be addressed before there is an increase in housing density.

The council response to these submissions, and many like them, is that there is capacity for more traffic, local projects will address any problems, and:

There is no linkage between the issues of over-crowding and quality of life.

The increase in density does not have a direct correlation to an increase in social problems, noise and desirability of the neighbourhood.

The rezoning proposal passes council at its November 2010 meeting, as if this increase in density is exempt from trends elsewhere. Here, reducing the space between people will not exacerbate noise and other problems or reduce the effect of cooling breezes, and local community projects can succeed in alleviating problems where governments have failed.

Epilogue ...

I travel to One Arm Point for work and stay in the home of a woman who makes radio broadcasts through Radio Goolarri. She knows everyone in my street, and she knows it would be good if our drug-dealer neighbour left.

One day, someone smashes through his front gates – in a pick-up truck in full-speed reverse – and a large man goes after him with a baseball bat. Our neighbour calls the police, then tells them to go away when he is less frightened and embarrassed at having called for help. It seems he sold an encumbered car to one of the biggest, and now crankiest, men in town. Soon after, at 3 a.m. one morning, someone sets fire to his car in the driveway. Our neighbour is not there; he is in the police lock-up for trouble earlier in the day. Police and firefighters arrive to deal with it. The volunteer firefighters bring their children and talk of the fishing trip they plan for later in the day. A community atmosphere prevails as many of us gather on the street. The fire is put out, the police and firefighters leave and we return to our homes and sleep.

We wake about an hour later to the sound of smashing windows and the glow of fire from next door. Molotov cocktails. I call the police; tell them I think that the house is now on fire. 'You're joking,' they say. They and the fire brigade return.

Our neighbour gets the message and leaves town. Two or three years later, I hear that he is dead. Shot, in a small town in Queensland.

The Broome council wants to clear up a wide stormwater drain that serves as a pathway in the neighbourhood for those who walk. The council's preferred method has been razing via bulldozer, all vegetation gone. Local residents have other ideas.

C___, who lives at the end of one of the streets and next to the drain/pathway, has planted trees and other natives there, slashes the grass when it needs to be cleared and collects the rubbish that blows in. At the beginning of this project, A___, who also lives next to this drain/pathway, stood in front of a council bulldozer, mobile phone held aloft, as it threatened a stand of trees. The bulldozer stopped, a discussion followed and the council has agreed not to raze the area. Now, with support from other people and organisations, C___ is making a park.

She says those in the neighbourhood not directly involved in the project respect it. There has been no vandalism, and little rubbish is left in the area. Once, when there was some trouble in the incipient park, the word went through the neighbourhood to make sure it doesn't happen again. Now, she has forty trees to water, and children playing in their shade ask her what she's doing.

'Just leave it. It's good the way it is,' says a man – drunk, eloquent, at home.

COLOUR IN THE FACE OF TIME
STEPHEN SCOURFIELD

It has been a day of colour. Not colour in one, overpowering sense but colour shifting every minute. This morning was cool and damp but with the promise of heat. It was platinum and squid ink; steel that's been heated and dipped in cold water. It was childhood cupboard-under-the-stairs dark, with the sterling glint of silverware in church. It was the ocean as tones of every-grey with wind moving it around. Light shafting down, god-like (whatever god), throwing silver on a random patch of ocean. It was stygian sea and lustrous splashes; sparkling fishes' gills and their dead, raven eyes. That was this morning on Montgomery Reef, four hundred square kilometres of sandstone that appears bizarrely from the ocean as the tide recedes.

At 2 a.m. this morning the reef was covered by nearly seven metres of bisquey sea, but now it is draining off in gentle waterfalls that tinkle like broken glass, jet in streams, and bring bursts of tiny fish to the white egrets standing alongside. They are usually here, waiting for this easy prey that comes draining off the reef after each tide; waiting for the supermarket to open.

We troll up the river, a channel that runs to the heart of Montgomery Reef, as the ocean drains and green turtles stick up their beaky faces to breathe.

Naturalist filmmaker David Attenborough once said that Montgomery Reef, twenty kilometres offshore from Talbot Bay, should be described as the Eighth Wonder of the World. And it certainly is a wonder, this picturesque cascade – a line of waterfalls out in the ocean, laid on for us, in our rubber Zodiacs, away from the expedition ship. High Cliffy Island borders the eastern edge of Montgomery Reef, and with the thought of this little island – one kilometre long and three hundred metres across, at its widest point, rising smartly from the sea to fifteen metres – vivid images from a 1929 Pathé newsreel flicker again through my mind. For High Cliffy Island was home to a physically impressive tribe of Aborigines called the Yawujibia, or Yawijibaya, who lived here, on and off, for 6,700 years. They were renowned as 'the giants of the north' – big, strong, perfectly adapted to their environment and, it is recorded, up to seven feet, or 2.1 metres tall. They rode mangrove rafts, in this massively tidal area, out to the island. Archaeologist Sue O'Connor has spent years researching the island and these people, and found evidence of stone house structures. It seems they might have stored freshwater in the dry season in large shells. Some time after the 1929 film was made the three-hundred-strong tribe disappeared. No one knows what happened to them, though there are tales of a big tidal wave and fatal conflict with neighbouring tribal groups. I have a copy of the rare and precious Pathé newsreel and see again, in my mind's eye, the heavily scarred men mock-charging the camera, spears held high.

The wind dies a little and we head back to the expedition ship through soupy, more-blue water, with frothy tops the white of altar-boy collars. I feel completely saturated by the place, the environment, the natural stupendousness of it, the intense salt, the omnipotent pressure of the pushing and drawing tide and of our natural part in it as complex fauna organisms; part of natural systems. By the time we reach the expedition ship, the day has changed. It is 10 a.m. and the sun has broken through, patchy at first. Some of the ocean is still a sable-blue, but some is now milky-turquoise, so you might think that parts are deep and parts shallow. You might think that we are in dangerous waters – that there is both sandy bottom and deep rocks. But that's not the case. It is just the clouds holding back the broad sunshine and letting it through windows. The sky matches it with both china blue and white and then the milky cusp of sky-through-cloud in between. It is a changeable moment, when either the clear-blue or the clouds might triumph. And then, bang, the sun wins and lays on an opaque, greenish-blue world, flat to the horizon. Yet even these are not the best of today's colour changes.

The ship is moved twenty kilometres to anchor off Raft Point, a dominating Kimberley sandstone bluff. On the other side of us is Steep Island, an equally sharp feature that fights for the eye's attention. The tideline moves up and down several metres, from dark and muddy, mussel-spangled rocks to the red Kimberley sandstone that was laid down two hundred million years ago. When we anchor, Raft Point is beige and tan with dark clefts of shadow, and looks somewhat benign. By 2 p.m., when we board Zodiacs to head to shore and Raft Point's art site, the colours have shifted to a resonating baked-red. It isn't hot today, but the rocks have known intense heat over millions of years. We land on the sand and shingle beach, where a bunch of personable boab trees looks for all the world like a family with foibles. It takes half an hour to climb a green gully to the art site. Several species of honeyeaters chorus around us, amid a whirr of rainbow bee-eaters' wings. The stories say that these dramatic, dark-eyed, mouthless Wandjinas control the clouds and the lightning, and by the time we get to them, it is overcast. They are happy we are here, says one of the people who has brought me; they have laid on some cloud for us. We sit and appreciate the moments and the images of Wandjinas, dugong, fish, snakes and yams. Tales both spiritual and practical. What we believe; what we eat. It is truth for traditional Aboriginal people here that Wandjina spirits created life and the land, and even the features of it, and control and bring the Wet season with its crucial rains, and gave instruction on how to live.

And then the sun bursts out. That's it, says my companion, they've had enough of us. We have had our moment and it's time to go. And we do, rock-hopping back to the now-languid sea. We board the Zodiacs and fumble with our bags, and I look up past the young crewman at the diesel outboard, to see the rock face has fired up to a rosy farewell. It looks fairground-happy. I snap a couple of pictures. It's 'can't-go-wrong stuff' as we pass in a big, white-waked arc past Raft Point. Picture Perfect indeed.

The day's colour has run the gambit of emotions – make 'em laugh, make 'em cry, pick 'em up, knock 'em down – and I head to my cabin to let it all settle not just in my head, but in the jangling cells of my body.

And then the ship swings on her anchor and there, outside the slide door and narrow balcony, Steep Island presents itself like a cut of fresh steak. My goodness, the rawness of that colour in the falling sun could make anyone grab a camera or a paint palette. And I step out and see Raft Point is doing the same. 'Anything you can do, I can do better.' The two of them out there together, facing off, pulsing. And then, surprisingly quickly, the sun dips to the horizon in a flashy, bloody dot, and vanishes, and all that's left is a murky purple and a memory of amber. I feel drained and washed out by the kaleidoscopic day.

The ship sails all night over water so salty that it seems to run an electrical charge, and in the morning we land in Vansittart Bay, where I walk the sandy crescent of it, then sit with my notebook, on a rock just above the shushing tideline and write, in the here-and-now. Not later, when I am in some other place; in this moment, where I am, when I am. I write in the present tense, for I am here now, and when you read it, it is this moment and you're in it too.

Writing 'plein-air'. This adjective, from the French 'en plein air' meaning 'in the open air', has come mostly to mean painting in the manner of the nineteenth century outdoors painters – a style which became central to French Impressionism. We accept that a painter will spend time in a place, viewing, absorbing, reacting, interpreting, and expressing this in the chemical moment when they are there. We accept that interpretation is the point that makes a watercolour painting other than a photograph. And, of course, we accept that the photograph relies totally on being somewhere, looking at something, if only for a fraction of a second. We go out to photograph, we go out to paint.

But writing is more about laptops (for me as a teenager, once the Remington Noiseless typewriter in the office, the Scheidegger portable on assignments from London to Germany), studies, retreats, and a garret. Writing plein-air challenges this – it is the note plucked and heard in the real world, not the musical chord that builds from later resonances.

And now I walk along hard flat sand on this Kimberley beach, by a Timor Sea of milky turquoise, pushed flat by still, warm weather, bejewelled by gently eroded shells. I write this, little notebook in hand, as it so often is out here in this office, this study, this studio. Why would I go somewhere else to record and describe this moment?

I see an ocean steely and mild under a ruffled sky. Rocks like crocs, sticking up thin, bony heads, which peer and disappear rhythmically with the almost imperceptible surge. Driftwood that could be bone, but too big. And the sighing, languid tideline.

I see lipstick-red coral in the sand, with miniscule organ pipes that might squeak a fugue. Two white shells, small as fingernails, perfectly paired. It occurs to me that there is a difference between the limpet crabs and the hermit crabs. The first hanging on in the moment, weathering out the ever-changing conditions, submerged, sunned, being there. The second scuttling away with carried baggage to a place made familiar and known.

I walk over a dune prickly with spinifex, to the salt lake behind, which floods under Wet season freshwater, inundated by two salty tides a day, and has big rocks in it, eroded to weird skulls.

The plane came down here, in this salt lake. The C-53 flying from Broome to Perth, way offcourse, lost and low on fuel, skidded to a death of sorts, its alloy bulk sacrificed. But we see it now for the strange luck it represents. Off bearing, in the dark, it landed lives in 1942. Eventually the crew and passengers were rescued, helped by Aboriginals who walked twenty kilometres from the Drysdale Mission. And now it gives a point of focus beyond the dune, over the salt lake, away from the beach in Vansittart Bay.

The ship moves us the short distance over to Jar Island, where we see Bradshaw or Gyorn Gyorn (also Gwion Gwion) rock art – active figures, figures with tassels and headdresses, elegant figures. I have been to the Kimberley more than fifty times and, on previous travels, Leah Umbagai, a talented painter and key figure in the Mowanjum arts community, explains that one of the Wandjinas, Namarali, was the life creator. 'He's like a god to us,' she says. He created the Gyorn Gyorn, which were hunters and gatherers. Three more Wandjinas came – one for each tribe – and gave law to each.

Jar Island's contemporary story is in its name, which is firstly for the earthenware remnants left by the seafaring Macassans, who sailed here from the straits between Borneo and Sulawesi. But that is only its very recent story. Jar Island's history goes back way before that. One needs to move the mind into the geological timescale to fully appreciate it. Begin with sand being laid millennia ago and compressed, several kilometres beneath the ocean's surface, to the Kimberley rock we see today. Back then, this land was all ocean bed – consider that, several hundred kilometres to the south, the Kimberley's Napier Range, which now stands as a sharp, tall feature beside the Gibb River Road, was once an underwater reef.

The water receded and, during the millennia that followed, Jar Island would have been a peak looking out on broad, productive valleys, grazed by many species of megafauna. I was recently in southern Africa, and it strikes me how these food-bowl valleys would have been such similarly populated landscapes to those that tore away from what is now Western Australia and ended up on the opposite side of the Indian Ocean. Humans, it is widely recognised, began their migration out of Africa, first northwards and then east to the Sahul continent, among other places. (A few days ago, in Arabia, I saw rare film of the Arabian Wolf, which looks very like the dingoes of Indonesia and now Australia.)

The arrival of Aboriginal people affected the landscape dramatically. It is widely thought that the first humans arrived in Australia between fifty and sixty thousand years ago, and that their arrival led to the extinction of the continent's megafauna. 'I've no doubt that people hunted them to extinction,' says mammalogist Tim Flannery, former Australian of the Year and a widely published author who has investigated this country's extinctions, past and present. The extinctions included up to twenty species of giant kangaroos, the marsupial lion and diprotodons – herbivorous marsupials as big as cows and resembling rodents. Which is interesting, because I might well be looking at one now. In red ochre on a wall inside a rock cave on Jar Island, the animal depicted looks very like the drawings of diprotodon that have been constructed through science and research.

Jar Island is another keystone in the rock art stronghold that is the Kimberley. There are whales, fish and an echidna, but it is the Bradshaw, or Gyorn Gyorn, that hold the attention. They commonly carry the name of Joseph Bradshaw as he was the first European to see and describe them, in 1891. Sight unseen, he had bought a million-acre Kimberley lease near what is now the

Prince Regent Nature Reserve for five hundred pounds. A wasp's nest on top of one Bradshaw painting has been dated, through optical stimulating luminescence, at seventeen thousand years old. Some, far inland, show ocean-going canoes with big prows. The link to cultures in Papua New Guinea has been proposed, as has that to African bushman art. I have travelled extensively in both places and clearly see these connections and echoes.

I don't see a 'land bridge' between Papua New Guinea and Australia, as it is often described. As I see it now, the two were really just part of the same landmass up until the end of the last ice age, ten to twelve thousand years ago. It has been reported that genetic research shows the common DNA of some New Guinean tribes and some Australian Aborigines. But after the land bridge was submerged and Australia became drier and hotter and New Guinea became wetter, differences developed.

Even within Bradshaw art there seem many styles – figures with tassels and tall headdresses, figures with yams (which are very important in Micronesian island culture), animated, active figures hunting, which are very reminiscent of the bushman art. I have seen this art in African caves, too, and to a vaguely educated eye, some is indistinguishable from active Bradshaw figures. Father Ernest Worms, an early stalwart of the Kalumburu Mission, near the north coast, learnt a lot of Aboriginal languages and recorded that he talked to local people about the Bradshaw galleries but they weren't able to explain them. I remember days when some Aboriginal people called Bradshaws 'rubbish art' or 'shit art' and painted over them. But some Kimberley Aboriginal tribes now claim Gyorn Gyorn art and incorporate it into their own canvas artworks. The story is told that Gyorn Gyorn is a local term for the sandstone shrike thrush, and Aboriginal legend says that the bird pecked at the rock until it damaged its beak, and then painted the figures with its feathers.

All of this runs through my mind in a clashing, confusing, demanding way as I climb among the caves and galleries of Jar Island. Who was here before me, for these many thousands of years? How did they live and what did the land look like? During the time of abundance, after the water level fell, the coast might have been one hundred kilometres from here. It was only after the end of the last ice age, and the inundation that ended the era of the Sahul continent perhaps only twelve thousand years ago – dramatically recently compared with the geological timescale we've been considering – that the Australian landmass was left looking much as it is today.

As the water rose, the food sources reduced – or, at least, changed. Jar Island became what it is: a touchstone not just of Aboriginal, but also of human history. A pretty island. A jumble of rocks and caves fringed by sandy beaches, surrounded by the turquoise water of the Timor Sea. A place that is awash in memories, and in shifting colour.

RIVER FEVER
LESLEY CORBETT

The eleven years I lived in the Kimberley were some of the most vivid of my life, not only because I fell in love and had my children there, but because something deep within me was nourished in a way that it hadn't been since leaving Zimbabwe. There is a brooding power in the African countries I grew up in, an almost palpable presence pulsing through the bush and beating out from the plains and rocks. I had not felt it again until I came to Derby to work for the Kimberley Land Council, but there it was, that same power emanating from the land, seeming to call to me, so that something within me unfurled and came alive. Some evenings I would leave the Land Council office and walk out on to the mudflats, listening to the birds calling down the night as the air slowly cooled. It was particularly beautiful up past the cemetery where boab trees stood in silhouette against the darkening sky. If I was lucky I might catch the heavy flight of a coucal moving between the bloodwoods and bauhinias, and oh how it lifted my spirits in those difficult days when the drilling rig was heading for Noonkanbah.

One day I discovered the river, and ever since I have had river fever. Nothing gladdens me more than to stand beside a waterhole on some quiet stretch of the Fitzroy and listen to the call of black cockatoos, the cracked laughter of kookaburras, the high haunting whistle of kite hawks. In such places a stillness steals over me, and I am filled with such wonder and contentment, it's as if I am witnessing the heartbeat of the world.

The man I fell in love with lived in Fitzroy Crossing, two hundred and sixty kilometres away. Most weekends one of us made the journey. Usually it was Steve, puttering along in his little Suzuki, still dusty from travelling the dirt roads to Noonkanbah where he was helping the community try to prevent mining on sacred land. One Saturday during the wet season it was my turn to do the drive. It had been raining heavily for days, and about halfway to Fitzroy Crossing I came to a long stretch of flooded road. I got out and tested the water that in some parts came up to my knees. For a while I stood in the midst of that vast plain and simply listened. It was utterly silent, no other vehicle for miles. There was the quiet ripple of water, a faint sighing of the wind in the grass, and now and then a bird piping liquid notes into the air. After a while a semitrailer came along, and the driver leaned out his window and greeted me. When I told him I'd never driven through water that deep before, he suggested I follow him through. We moved in slow stately procession through the floodway, then I continued on, in a hurry now to see my fella.

The Fitzroy River wound through our lives. For a

while Steve and I lived on its banks in a caravan. We got flooded out that year, the river rising higher than people had ever seen. At night we heard the terrible cries of cattle being swept downstream. Each morning Steve put a stick at the edge of the floodwaters, and each day they crept closer, until finally they engulfed our van, forcing us to take shelter with some friends.

As the river rose and spread across the landscape it became clear why Fitzroy Crossing was built in a series of scattered settlements. The town had fractured into islands of high ground separated by long stretches of muddy water. To get from one area to another you either waded, if it wasn't too deep, or you found someone with a boat. Snakes, spiders and goannas clung to the tops of submerged trees, while cattle bellowed mournfully, stranded on little patches of disappearing land.

By now the entire town was cut off. Great chunks had been eaten out of the bridge across Brooking Channel, and Plum Plain was under water. Road trains couldn't get through from Perth or Darwin, and supplies had to be brought in by air.

At the height of the floods we walked down to the main bridge and watched the river thundering down. It was an awesome sight, a mighty untamed creature filled with power that seemed intent on drowning all the land. Tragically some old people in one of the outlying communities lost their lives in the floodwaters when their boat overturned.

Fitzroy Crossing's water supply had become contaminated, and all across town people were falling ill with dysentery. Steve was one of them. For days he curled up at our friend's house, miserably clutching his stomach, and so when the floodwaters finally receded, the kindy teacher helped me clean the mud out of the van.

Our first child was conceived while we were living on the banks of the river. As my belly swelled into glorious new lines we decided not to risk being flooded out again. Housing was impossible to find in Fitzroy, so we moved to the tiny settlement of Camballin, with the river only a short drive away. Every chance we could we went fishing and swimming there, until the wet season set in and the road became impassable except to four-wheel drives. Amidst the tic tic of cicadas the spear-grass grew tall, and the plains turned a luminous green. Storm clouds swelled on the horizon, and our skin had a perpetual sweaty sheen.

Late one afternoon as sun tipped the spinifex with gold, I walked across the plain towards the Looma hills, feeling the pulse of the land and the powers slumbering within it. For a long time I stood there, calling out to the spirits of the land, asking them to protect the precious child I carried.

He was born early in February. By then floodwaters had crept over some of the roads around Camballin, and were lapping at several houses, but the main road remained open. When my waters broke we had to drive thirty kilometres along a corrugated dirt road, then another eighty kilometres of bitumen to reach Derby, the nearest town. We needn't have hurried. It was eighteen hours before he arrived and transformed our lives.

When we came home, we took him down to the river and dipped his feet in it, a kind of baptism, letting the water sing its way into his veins. We did the same with our second child. We were living back in Fitzroy Crossing when I became pregnant with him, and this time it was to Donkey Crossing I went, begging the river spirits to protect the little one nestled within me.

Not long after our second son was born we moved into a house of our own on a bush block near Derby filled with ghost gums, boabs, and bauhinias. It was a beautiful place to live, watching the seasons change and the clouds roll in. When the rains came we would dance out in them, and afterwards the kids would splash in the muddy pools and hurl mud at each other, the red becoming impregnated in their clothes. Sometimes we drove to Willare Bridge and watched the river rise, the boys delighting in flinging themselves into the gentler side currents and letting themselves be swept along. The best times though were during the dry season when we returned to our old haunts along the river. We would drive home in the dark, keeping a watchful eye out for cattle, still tasting the bream and cherrabun we had cooked over a fire. The slow murmuring song of the river ran through our dreams, calling us to return again and again.

I grew up with the seasons arranged the way they are in the Kimberley, where the rains fall during the time of greatest heat. Something elemental rebels in me when the seasons are reversed as they are in Perth, where rain falls cold and bleak through the long winter months, and never invites you to dance in it. I doubt I'll ever get used to it. Leaving the Kimberley was agony. Driving away from our house, my heart was crying out, begging me not to do this. A dull despair entered me as we turned south off the Broome Highway.

We live now on a bush block in the Perth hills with a winter creek filled with frog-song, but for years I mourned the Kimberley and felt hopelessly uprooted. In time I grew more contented, and learned to accept that there will always be this hollow place within me, this spirit longing. If I don't dwell on it, it dies down to a faint whimper rather than a roar that drowns out my life.

I went back a few years ago, flying into the arms of that beloved country, shedding tears of joy at sight of the first boab tree, my first glimpse of the river. As I lay beside my man that night in the glow of the campfire, the bright Kimberley stars reflected in the water, I was the richest woman on earth.

SACRED EARTH AND ANCESTRAL GIFTS
PAT MAMANYJUN TORRES

What is this notion of a Sacred Earth and what makes the earth sacred to our families? What are the ancestral gifts that we have received from generations of my immediate families? When I speak about the Sacred Earth and the ancestral gifts I am divulging the belief systems and philosophies of our family to take readers on a journey. It is a private and intimate exposing of our religious beliefs in the public domain. Like other people around the world, we have our ways of seeing, naming and understanding the universe. If I share some of my beliefs, I trust you will receive the knowledge of these gifts and handle them with respect. We will travel through my family's diverse Australian heritage so I can convey something about the forming of my immediate families' Indigenous identity through at least six generations. The sharing of our families' personal boogarri or dreamings, and through it the sacred connection we have to several places in the West Kimberley, its environments, specific plants, animals and people, shows knowledge of our relationship to the sacred earth and the ancestral gifts bestowed upon us through our kinship groups, rayi-spirit and boogarri connections. These provide the emotional and spiritual food we need to create a healthy spiritual mind and physical body. This knowledge is given with positivity and good liyan – inner feelings – to create better understandings and relationships between people. Remember this: if knowledge is used wrongly or misrepresented the spirits of country take action, so walk with love and peace in your heart not greed and hate. Rightful action and good heart sustains us all.

My elders teach that Dreaming Ancestors from boogarri.garra created our environment and handed down the sacred stories that explain our ways of looking at the world. In the past our stories were told in our own languages. Language is a powerful tool for identity: it carries the ideas that describe our view of the world and the journeys of ancestral beings are found embedded in the language names of places. The word boogarri means dreams, and boogarri.garra is a way of seeing the world: a time of creation informing our Dreaming histories, a collection of secret, sacred and public stories explaining when and why the earth, its environments and its animals and people took form. It is our belief and knowledge system: our traditional ecological science, our way of measuring and evaluating the world.

We also have concepts about land in our languages that link us to our clan country, such as burru that means place, clan country, family estate or home-country. In this idea we have notions such as ningam which is the female line and borr which is the male line. Borr cannot exist without ningam; male cannot exist without female, and female cannot exist without male. These notions create balance in the Indigenous world and are embedded with layers of meaning that bring ancient rules of respect and responsible action for individual, family and community. Ningam and borr is one way of defining our 'sense of belonging' and through remembering language we celebrate our reconnection to traditional country.

So here begins a small segment of my family's story of identity and sense of belonging with the sacred earth and the ancestral gifts we possess from our connections.

I am a traditional owner and direct descendant of the Torres and Drummond families of the Broome and Dampier Peninsular regions from the West Kimberley. My rayi-spirit (spirit child, or soul-body), comes from Manalagun, the freshwater place near the Foreshore Beach on Jugun country between Jirrigun and Jiljirrigun. These places are on the songline tracts of the Three Sisters and the Dog-man Dreaming. My conception totem is birrali, the yellow sand cockle. My skin-group is Banaga. It includes the brolga, gudurru.warrany, as its special animal. My jalnga, or spirit power, is Gujarra Bulany, the double rainbow snake. My Aboriginal name is Mamanyjun, a red coastal berry. An aunt, now deceased, gave this name to me. She told me that I was Jugun-ngany and Yawuru-ngany but also not to forget that I was Jabirr Jabirr-ngany too. She called me 'mamanyjun seed from Winnawaalborr' as acknowledgment of my families' connection to northern Jabirr Jabirr lands. My families relate to several Indigenous language groups in the West Kimberley, including the Jugun and Julbayi Yawuru of the Broome region, and the Jabirr Jabirr and Nyul Nyul of the Dampier Peninsular region. My Torres side of the family has connections with southern Jabirr Jabirr through our male ancestor Milare, aka Wallamarra, whose clan country begins at Gon.ganada near Minariny, north of Prices Point; and through our female ancestor Keleregodo, aka Kilibin, who is from Winnawaal and the Nyirriny.nyin.gan water place, of east Sandy Point to northern Jabirr Jabirr. We also have Spanish-Filipino heritage through the marriage between Manila-man, Catalino Torres, and Tiolbodonger, Matalja or Matilda, who is the sister of Remi Balgai. He was commonly known as Irrami. Many of our ancestors' names become lost in the pages of history but it was explained to me that it was normal cultural practice for family members to take on another name within their lifetime when other family members died with the same personal name. This was done as a sign of respect for deceased people as others were not allowed to voice the name of a deceased person, as it would invoke the dead spirit. So the name nyabaroo (sometimes spelt nyapuru, or known as kumunyjayi) is used to refer to the person who has the name of a deceased person until a new name is given. Some families still follow this tradition today.

My Drummond family has Scottish and Irish ties from male ancestors from the early pastoral industry, and the Javanese man Drummond who arrived for the pearling industry. My female great-grandparents – known as

Tiolbodonger, aka Matalja or Matilda, from Jabirr Jabirr, Nyul Nyul heritage; and Miwarl, aka Mary Minyal, from Jugun and Yawuru heritage – were the first Indigenous women who married men of different cultural heritage. Our families have since intermarried men and women from many nations but my family members passionately identify as Indigenous Australians. This form of self-identification is a product of past Australian policies, combined with our own choice based on our cultural heritage.

I am now an elder-woman and a grandmother. I have five adult children and four grandchildren, each of whom have an Indigenous name, a skin-group, a rayi-spirit, and a jalnga. My children are Garimba skin-group because I am a Banaga woman. My mother is also Garimba and my mother's mother is Banaga. The mothers determine the children's skin-group, so my sons' children will have a different skin-group to my daughter's children. The mothers of my sons' children must fit into the Balyjarri skin-group so their children will be Burungu. My daughters' children will be Banaga.

In pre-colonial times my ancestors from Nyul Nyul and Jabirr Jabirr – the Jugun and Yawuru people – had detailed knowledge of kinship systems and other respect systems that ordered our society. This nila-ngany, our knowledge system, formed rules for living that related people, places, animals, plants, land and sea environments and the heavens above into a close and interdependent living system. Ancestors too had their own dreaming, skin groups and connections to specific places which continue in this century to be interconnected by our families.

What I am sharing here is knowledge about how kinship binds us to our ancestors, the sacred dreaming places, animals of the sea, land and sky and to environments and weather conditions. If you are connected to a special place, or a particular animal or plant, it is your responsibility to learn the stories of place, protect it and maintain its story and its environment. In the past we had stories that were told, songs that were sung, dances celebrated and body paints and adornments placed on people and items as part of our celebration to bring the spirits of country to life and renew the earth and environment. We are the guardians of the sacred earth and of the sacred knowledge that maintains balance in our world, it is we who sing up the country and bring it to life.

My first experience with Aboriginal sciences and sacred knowledge as ancestral gifts began when I became sick with tetanus. My great-grandfather, jalbi (to signify his great-grandfather status) Karim Drummond, a jalnga. ngurru man, gave me a gift of the 'healing power of emu' through an emu chick spirit. I learned that it would grow with me, protecting and guiding my way in the world. I remember seeing the small golden-white feathers cupped in his hands and heard the chirping sound of a baby emu chick. I was only two years old at the time. The pure wonderment and fascination I felt for this proud and strong man of culture is with me still. His old and frail body held the mugudal or body scars of past rites of manhood. His nose and ears had piercings through them for placing carved bone items that showed his level of knowledge and achievements as a man of high degree. Jalbi Karim shared with me the Jugun stories for children about Marala the Emu-man, Yung.gorayi.gorayi the Rainbow Serpent, Jindirrabirrbirr the Mudlark man and other strange and magical creatures like the Goomboon, a mangrove being. These stories were later retold by my elder-women relatives. He talked about rayi-spirits living in our land, that the rayi-spirits are like the spirit of children yet to be born; it is in essence our inner soul or psyche. If you kill the rayi-spirit or soul-body of a person you also kill the person. So we must build people with a strong sense of self and connectedness to their clan country. Their connections are derived even before birth.

Many of my family members validate and respect the gift of being able to 'dream' and pick up on the energies within a person or place. This knowing has guided relationships within our families. The ability to dream our future children and see future events through visions is part of the ancestral gifts held within contemporary Kimberley Indigenous families. These gifts combine with ethical and respectful practice, and form part of our sacred knowledge that we protect and maintain today.

So how are our children born to us? How are their identities formed? Well, often we have dreams of our future children and see their physical shape, hair colour, personality and gender, way before a child is born. Rayi-spirit places exist on the land and the land under the sea where they wait patiently for the rightful mother. I have seen my children's rayi appear to me in dreams soon after they were conceived. My second daughter dreamt her children years before they were born. In my dreams, I am shown how each child is connected to place, animal and environment. Often the rayi spirit-child is seen in dreams as a toddler-child of eighteen months in age. These are some of the dreams I have had of my own children before they were born.

Milangka, my first child, was first seen as a nimanburr or fruit bat hanging on a boab tree at Lirrigun, near Ganin in Broome. She appeared as a nimanburr hanging downwards towards the ground, then released herself from the branches, turned a somersault and landed on the ground changing into a female child with curly hair and a happy, laughing face. I saw her face, the dark skin and body shape. Later my mother and I dreamt Milangka walking along with a white lion on a grassy plain. The lion totem is from her fathers' country, Tanzania, Africa. So Milangka has three gifts: the fruit bat, the boab tree and the African white lion. Milangka is a highly creative person and has a fascination for African spiritual knowledge.

Yunimirdi, my second child, was seen playing with Barjida the Northern Quoll and a small whip snake among seed grasses. His place is called Mamabulanjin and it is the current site of the Imamabulanjin Resource Centre in Broome. I saw the rayi of a small boy child playing with the small whip snake and Barjida among the grasses on the sun-bleached pindan sands. When workers started to build on this site in the mid 1980s, my child was often sick. The illness ceased when the building project finished. Yunimirdi is a skilled hunter and gatherer of bush foods.

Mowangka, my third child, was conceived after my husband had shot a freshwater crocodile at Dowidiya, south of Fitzroy Crossing. The wounded animal floated straight into my arms at the side of the river where I was collecting gagarru, the freshwater mussels: this was an extraordinary event that signified something special. Some months later I was pregnant and my Gooniyandi cousins' grandparents explained the significance of this event. They gave my daughter her freshwater name, Dowidiya, and her totem is gwaniya, the freshwater crocodile. Later into my early pregnancy I dreamt of finding a large black-lipped oyster on a rock when I was fishing with my mother at Jungku, the site of the ancestral Three Sisters at Riddell Beach in Broome. This was the place where the Gurdidi Ngunu lit the first fire to cook their fresh fish whilst they hid from Bugu-wamba, the Giant Dog-man. I saw this beautiful oyster on the rock and began to hit it with a large rock so that I could eat the food. When my child was born she had a lump on the side of her head, which made me panic, thinking that something was wrong. My mum told me that it was her baanmaan, a physical sign that my daughter had been marked when I hit the oyster on the large rock. So Jarr.ngan, the black-lipped oyster is her special saltwater totem. She is like myself having both fresh and saltwater totems and her rayi-spirit comes from Jungku the fire-place of the ancestral women that we call Gurdidi Ngunu. Mowangka does not like eating oysters but she will eat most other seafood. She has a great gift for dreams, visions and artwork.

Mowandi is my fourth child. My dream showed my great-grandfather as a warrior standing in front of me handing me a boy child over a small river that had smooth stones and freshwater running into a sandy pool near the coast. He called out the name of the place, as Wadu.gudu. and he gave me a name for my child that I could not pronounce, so I named my child after him instead. As my great-grandfather handed me the child, a large king brown snake, Wirril, slithered between our legs and lay across the freshwater stream. I knew this child and the king brown snake had a special connection. Later we also connected the small gurlibil, or sea turtle, to him as well. My cravings were for vegetable foods and minimal meat during this pregnancy. Mowandi respects cultural ways and has a strong inner power like the king brown snake.

My last child, Matalja, is connected to the giant waterlily with the upturned leaves and two giant lingurra, saltwater crocodiles. I first saw her in a dream as I walked along the banks of a deep saltwater creek near the junction of three rivers with a freshwater lake nearby. I remember seeing the beautiful colours of the waterlily first and then this small girl rayi followed me up the hill along the top of a rocky cliff. When I glanced over my shoulders there appeared two giant saltwater crocodiles swimming towards each other and crossed over in front of me. I could feel the power of the crocodiles as they looked towards me holding their gaze whilst they swam past. I remember eating so much meat during this pregnancy. Matalja has so much inner strength and beautiful ways of relating to people.

I now have four grandsons who have their own rayi-spirit places in Jabirr Jabirr and Jugun country. They have their own jalna connected to multicoloured dogs and dingoes, olive sea snake and yellow speckled sea-snake, whales and green sea turtle. They have been given their Indigenous names and will know their kinship names and jalnga as they grow older. As I explained earlier, my daughters' children have the same skin-group as mine, which is Banaga and my son's children have the skin-group name of Balyjarri.

My mother's ningam is located in Jugun and Yawuru country and my mother's borr is located at Winnawaal in Jabirr Jabirr country. Her rayi is from Winjal.ngan in Jugun country, her birth totem is the catfish and her jalnga includes Bidjada the Emu and many snakes including Wulgudany the One-eyed snake, Baninyburr the Black-headed snake, Wirril the King-brown snake. My brother Jowandi has children whose rayi-spirits come from Jabirr Jabirr country connecting them to green frog, sea eagle, red-bellied black snake, and sea snakes. His totem is Baninyburr the Python.

We are living in the twenty-first century, a highly technological age of humankind. So why is it that we still have a fascination for the notion of a sacred earth? Despite huge advances in technology humans still reach for something intangible and more than material items. They reach for a spiritual connection to place, a sense of belonging and reasons for living. These reasons may be found in our concepts such as boogarri, rayi, jalnga ningam and borr, concepts handed down from our ancestors to our families today. These beliefs and ways of being have survived many historical events experienced in the last two hundred years of contact with kartiya, or white people. Kartiya scholars have described boogarri. garra as The Dreaming: it is about our religion, laws and rules for life. The Dreaming is both past and present; if we grasp it with both hands, and with our minds and spirit, it can influence our future; it is circular, a never-ending concept of time. The knowledge of our early peoples, our dreaming ancestors and the interrelated connections through our individual rayi-spirit child, its jalnga or power, and boogarri – its dreamings – is what makes us unique beings.

The connections that humans have with other humans, animals of the sea, the land and sky, are integral to the ancestral gifts we still hold close to our hearts. If we embrace it with our contemporary lives and inform our minds and our hearts we are enriched by its teachings. We feel fully connected to our clan country. The special relationship that Indigenous Australian people have with the earth and all beings that live on it is what makes the earth sacred to us. Our families have taught us we must live with the cycles and seasons of the earth taking only what was needed for good health and spiritual wealth. This is our way of living sustainably on this land.

LEAF
SANDY TOUSSAINT

I am crouching on a sandy bank of the Fitzroy River in the Kimberley with several Walmajarri women and men. We are fishing. Ngunta, a 'sister' and friend to me, is a few metres away, her hand-held line drifting the water for unsuspecting fish. Ngunta's mother Walka is upstream with her own line and buckets ready. Marminjiya, Ngunta's daughter, and her husband Jimmy, a Gooniyandi man, are in a small boat further down the river. They have strong lines and rods for barramundi. Jane, one of my kartiya friends, is thousands of kilometres away, down south in urban Perth. But a leaf, which catches my eye as it floats in the shallow water, reminds me of her. Leaves, in various colours, textures and ages, are a form of attachment and silent communication between us.

The leaf is from a majala tree, a freshwater mangrove known to local Aboriginal people as a source of medicine. There are many majala trees along the river. Their leaves, in different stages of life and death, are everywhere. The leaf that catches my attention is beautifully variegated; delicate but strong. I pluck the leaf from the water and lay it beside me. It stays there for many hours while we continue to fish in the harsh, dry heat. Ngunta, always a fine fisher, catches six bream, a catfish and a swordfish; Marminjiya and Jimmy secure several large barramundi. Walka catches a number of bream. Two cherrabun and one bream are my contribution. At dusk we head back to our camp to light the fire, cook the fish, and settle in for the night.

Marminjiya and Jimmy bring the boat alongside where Ngunta and I are fishing. It is a small boat so we travel back to our camp in parties of two. Jimmy is at the helm. Marminjiya alights in order for Ngunta and me to board the boat. Jimmy skillfully guides the boat away from the bank. As he does so, I realise that I have forgotten the leaf. I call out to Marminjiya, 'I left that leaf, that majala leaf behind!' Ngunta, now beside me, says, 'Don't worry ngapurlu ... there's plenty more ... don't worry, we'll get another leaf.' At the same time, Marminjiya, waiting at the water's edge, calls, 'Don't worry, there's plenty more leaves around.' Despite their reassurances, and my own awareness of the abundance of leaves, somehow a form of attachment has evolved between the leaf on the sandbank and me. The leaf represents distant places and conversations. I call out again, 'My friend in Perth would like that leaf ... I want that leaf for her.' Marminjiya, with guidance from Ngunta, finds the leaf, picks it up, holds it high and yells, 'I've got that leaf, and I'll take it back to camp.'

Ngunta guts the large barramundi, encases it in damp paperbark, ties it with twine stripped from a local tree, and bakes it in an earth oven. I hear Marminjiya's voice as she returns to the camp, 'There's that leaf for you. I'll leave it in the pannikin ... it will be right there.'

We consume the smoked barramundi, bread, potatoes, and billycan tea for dinner, and talk quietly for a while by the fire in the darkness. Some wood is left smouldering to discourage mosquitoes and other insects. We unroll our swags and prepare for sleep.

Jane meets me at the airport when I fly back to Perth three weeks later. We go to my house and enjoy cups of tea, and share some of the home-baked damper Ngunta has sent home with me. Ngunta, Marminjiya and family are now thousands of kilometers away, although they are very much on my mind. I give Jane the partially dried leaf –

LEAF CARRIES ITS PLACE WITH IT
JANE MULCOCK

Kimberley leaf carries its place with it ...
In its colour, in its symmetry, in its fractured, brittle,
fragile truth.

Fell from its branch to become ... the bearer of another
time, fresh and splendid and beautiful ... through the air
spinning in the afternoon.

Touches the river's cool surface, spreading the slightest
ripple, like a story, like a messenger, ready for the next
road.

(As it fell it captured the sunlight on the water, through
the trees it captured laughing voices, insect calls, smoky
tea, the intimacies of silence, the delicate, delicate
wholeness of being there, like a photograph, inscribed
with memory.)

And your face dancing with the light of being there as well, when the leaf fell ... is like a portal to that riverbank, like a room of softly sketched images conjuring up a gentle moment.

SEAGULL
PAT LOWE

Something white was tumbling in the road, amongst the traffic of afternoon shoppers. A seagull, injured by a careless car. I swung onto the central verge and parked. The bird flapped and toppled between the cars then came to rest near the kerb. People went by, not noticing. Moving slowly, I came up behind the bird. It sat hunched, misshapen, its head turned back to look at me. I stood still a moment, then crouched down close behind it. The seagull watched me, still without moving. I made a quick lunge and seized it in both hands. It struggled then, and tried to peck me, but I had my hands over its wings and behind its neck, where its bill couldn't reach. One wing was broken at the shoulder, and I folded it back as carefully as I could against the seagull's body. In its pain or terror, eyes wild, the captured bird bit savagely again and again at the injured wing.

I stood up in the indifferent street holding the bird in front of me. Near my car I hesitated. Next to me, two young people were getting into a Moke. I looked at them in appeal, and the young man asked if he could help. We discussed possibilities while his girlfriend in the driver's seat looked bored. I asked him to find me a box.

The young man walked towards a shop and I sat on the side of the Moke, still holding the seagull. I made an attempt to speak to the young woman driver, but she only glanced at me and didn't answer. We waited in silence. Her companion came back with a small cardboard box into which I carefully placed the gull, then shut down the flaps. The couple drove away.

At the pensioners' quarters I exchanged greetings with the fat old dog that lives there, then stood looking at the aviary of recovering birds, mostly parrots injured by boys with shanghais, and waited for Len to come out.

'There's nothing much I can do for a seagull,' Len said. 'I've tried that many times, but they always die. I don't think they can tolerate captivity.'

I nodded.

'The best thing you can do is to leave it in its own territory, near the sea. I used to take seagulls down to Crab Creek, away from cats and children, and release them there.'

What happens to them then, I wanted to know. I supposed they died.

'No, the wing can heal,' Len assured me. I showed surprise. 'Oh yes, the wing can heal. It droops a bit, but the bird can still fly.'

I didn't think that would be likely for this seagull, its wing hanging loose from the shoulder like a torn sleeve, but I said nothing more.

I took the seagull home and opened the lid of its box. The bird had turned around in the small space, and its wing had twisted in front of its body, grotesque as an elbow bent the wrong way. I rearranged the wing along its side. My dog was curious but responded to my warning. Sensing a journey, he jumped into the back of my car. Together we set out for Crab Creek.

By now the sun was getting low and it shone into my eyes until I reached the turn-off, where the road heads south onto the open plain. From there you can see right across to the horizon. I drove along the salty-white marsh road, which the seawater seeps into and floods at highest tides, to the line of scrub where pindan meets the salt flats and the track turns red.

The road then winds along the coast, and short tracks here and there lead to the low red cliffs above the beach. I took the second turn, where a single tree stands overlooking the rocks. The tide was out.

I picked up the seagull in its box and carried it down to place it on the sand. To avoid handling the bird again, I pushed down the bottom flaps of the box and lifted it away, leaving the gull resting on the sand. At once the seagull struggled to fly. It lurched forward, tumbled and fell. I realised then that it had other injuries besides its broken wing. It seemed unable to stand upright. It tumbled again, fell on its back, and righted itself. My dog reached out his neck and sniffed, intrigued, but I called him away.

From a short distance I stood, uncertain, watching the crippled seagull. Should I leave it there, helpless? Or should I kill it quickly – bludgeon it to death with a piece of driftwood or put it back in its box and set it down in front of the wheel of my car, and drive over it? Who is to say that a sudden, brutal death is better than a slow and lingering one? Aboriginal people I know are repelled by so-called mercy killing. 'Letim die self,' they say. There is a right time to die and animals, like human beings, 'die when they're ready'.

The seagull wasn't ready to die; that was certain. It resisted fiercely the threat it felt from me, and from my dog. Yet it would die if I left it, and the suffering might be worse.

The sun went down, golden. The shadow of approaching night rose in the east. I started to move away. The crippled seagull, like a fallen ballet dancer, lay enveloped in its broken wing, pure white, alone on the darkening beach.

The next day I thought again about the seagull. When afternoon came and work was over I drove back across the salty plains to Crab Creek. The sun was higher over the flat country than it had been when I crossed the day before. The tide again was low.

I walked slowly along the stretch of beach where I had left the seagull, then out onto a rocky spit among the mangroves. I kept a lookout for the grey, sodden body I half expected to find in place of the gleaming ballet dancer of the day before.

I turned south then, along the shoreline. A white shape amongst the mangrove roots caught my attention until it became a plastic bag. I moved up to the high-water mark.

A few steps along, scattered about with other tidal debris, lay some feathers. They were spread over several yards of beach, still freshly white. I picked up a small cluster of curly down, as yet untouched by the tide.

It was easy to make out the spot where the bird had been dismembered. The scattered plumage converged on a denser hub, around which the sand was patterned with small, fine traces of living things. In between crab tracks, and others I couldn't decipher, I recognised the claw marks of a bird of prey. I looked around for a body, but there was none. Amongst the debris rustled hermit crabs, busy with the little that remained.

Looking more carefully, I found the delicate bones of a bird's leg. The broken joint was still moist and red, the foot folded down like an empty glove. I picked up the bone and pressed its glove against the sand. The toes splayed out to form the webbed foot of a seagull.

SANDY'S SEND-OFF
MURRAY JENNINGS

SCENE: Halls Creek Cemetery, the afternoon of
           the first of May, 1994. Clear blue sky,
           warm sun, gentle breeze; no humidity.
           The funeral of Alexander (Sandy) Taylor.

COLIN: Okay Muz, synchronise watches. You got
           3.30?

ME: Spot on.

COLIN: Great. Now, you okay with the walkie-
           talkie?

ME: I think so. But can we run through it again
           to make sure?

COLIN: No worries. The others are set to go. They
           get your call; they take off.

The 'others'? Two young pilots belted into the cockpits of two Cessnas on the Halls Creek airstrip, engines idling. One of the men was in Sandy's own plane. He was the soon-to-be son-in-law of the man we were about to farewell, half a kilometre away, as the crow – or Cessna – flies. This was precision stuff. I was unfamiliar with walkie-talkies, but having spent most of my career in radio studios, working to the clock, I wasn't bothered. I was more concerned with saying the right things in the graveside tribute speech I'd been asked to deliver, hoping I wouldn't get tearful in the company of the expected fifty or so people who were already entering the cemetery, and to whom funerals were not unusual. I needed to be in control. I was to put out the call to the pilots, just as I was commencing my speech, timed to last between five and six minutes, giving them time to take off, circle, then zoom over us, dipping their wings in a fly-past, in honour of the late, much-loved Sandy Taylor. Sandy's widow, Libby, had prepared a program for the 4 p.m. graveside service to follow the 2 p.m. requiem mass in St Mary's church. My copy of the program looked like this:

At the Graveside
Sandy Taylor
1. Prayers: Bishop Jobst
2. First Reflection: Peter
3. Second Reflection: Manita
4. Tribute by Murray + coordinating fly-past in honour of Sandy

5. Coffin is lowered
6. Family sprinkle rose petals
7. The grave is filled in.

I had scribbled walkie-talkie instructions next to that, and, at the bottom, my ad lib points, in case my nerves got the best of my memory:

A transplanted Yorkshireman ... his recognition of this 'spirit country' ... I've known him for only nine months, we clicked quickly ... he's been a good friend ... TV days ... Sandy had worked in TV studios ... we'd swapped yarns ... warm, generous, repaired my cassette player free of charge ... great sense of humour ... a close family, Libby and three daughters ... popular in HC, he's sorted some technical problems at PRK ... Sandy's two dreams ... to see the airport sealed ... and the Halls Creek region officially renamed Yarleyel out of respect for the Kija and Jaru people ...

I read it again and my mind wanders in the comparative silence of the wind, the soft scraping of shoes on the gravel and the solemn whispers of the arriving mourners, Kija, Jaru and kartiya. W.H. Auden's 'Twelve Songs' comes to mind. A stopped clock, a coffin, and aeroplanes above us ... And I wonder if those lines had been in Libby's mind. No. Auden's last line was too negative. Libby is a strong, positive person. And I feel sure that she will survive this. Then a voice in my head cries, 'Stop the watches and rewind the tape!' Alone at night, I'd been reading Bruce Chatwin, wondering why he left the question mark off his book title *What Am I Doing Here*. I asked myself the question and came up with *forestalling early retirement*. I scratched that out and substituted *escaping the clutches of a tyrannical boss down in Perth*. But there was more to it than that. The lure of my escape route had been too strong to resist. A sort of secondment from the Australian Broadcasting Corporation to a temporary position of broadcast trainer with Puranyangu-Rangka Kerrem, or Radio PRK, the Halls Creek station in the Kimberley Aboriginal Broadcasting Network, which includes stations in Broome, Fitzroy Crossing and Kununurra. So *I'm here because they needed someone and I thought I could help* ... Yes, but also *I'm here because, quite simply, I am yet another city person who fell in love with the Kimberley, at first sight*.

And what did it for me? In the early 1970s, I arrived riding high in the cab of a semitrailer with Bill, a truckie, up the Great Northern Highway for a three-week holiday organised by my father-in-law, Duncan Ord, then Manager of the Derby Meat Processing Company (DEMCO). That trip was eventful enough, a real eye-opener for a southern city boy, even one used to roughing it in cold winter jarrah and karri forests. Lots of cursing at caravanning grey nomads with their headlights on high beam, Bill throwing on his roof-mounted spot that all but melted the oncoming vehicles until they dropped their lights. Lots of beers, stopping at Sandfire Flat in its rougher days, joining a truckies' school in the little bar, lots of laughs when another truckie's blue heeler sat on a bar stool and 'yodelled' to the choruses of 'Pub With No Beer'. There is a lot of rain, with a great deal of mud and sliding along the unsealed road to the coastal highway. Eventful? If I'd said that to Bill, I can hear his response: 'You ain't seen nothin' yet, mate!'

Am I there yet? Is this the Kimberley? Well, yes, but ... it's Broome, pre–Lord McAlpine, few tourists, a fascinating racial mix, the Japanese cemetery, the old luggers in the mangroves, the roar of the public bar of the Roebuck Bay Hotel, Chinatown, the Sun Pictures building, forlorn, neglected, not yet revived. I am wide-eyed and fascinated with the physical history of the town we'd been taught about in primary school. But it wasn't until Duncan took me to Derby that I could feel I was really at the frontier of another country. Meeting and drinking with locals, both Caucasian and Aboriginal, a barbeque, munching slabs of mangrove crab washed down with cold beers, sitting on the end of the Derby jetty at sunset, marvelling at the Boeing 747 vapour trail bisecting the crescent moon and Venus. Windjana Gorge, freshwater crocs at my feet on the sandy shore of the creek, overlooked by high rocky crags. Then on up the Derby–Gibb River Road to Glenroy Homestead and an overnight stay at Mt House Station where Duncan had lived for many seasons as the refrigeration engineer for the Air Beef Scheme. Being wined and dined by the management, hearing of its imminent demise as the absentee beef moguls were making changes to the industry that had so transformed the Kimberley since the days of the Duracks and Forrests. All this had merely whetted my appetite and I knew that I was going to return one day ...

Through the 1980s and early 1990s, I visited several times, as co-compere and a judge for the annual Derby Country Music Festival, even broadcasting the ABC's 'Country Calling' show out of an old caravan sitting slightly off the vertical in the red dust of the rodeo ground. Our signal went out to the rest of Western Australia via a satellite dish mounted on a trailer next to the caravan. A bizarre set-up anywhere else, but in the Kimberley, this was perfectly normal. And the people! Music broke down any barriers that might have existed. We were treated like royalty. One night, after the concert had finished and we were packing up the gear, I was crossing the rodeo ground when a hand grabbed my shoulder. 'Hey, Murray Jennings.' I turned around and recognised one of the singer-songwriters who had entertained us earlier in the day. 'I'm Geoff Fletcher, you know?' I nodded and we shook hands. Then he leaned in close to my ear and started to sing softly. It was a song he was writing about a windmill, 'Southern Cross'. He needed some help with a rhyme and asked me if I could help. I can't remember if he used my suggestion, but this was the beginning of a lifelong friendship. Geoff was from Halls Creek, one of the many Kija people trucked unceremoniously off their traditional country enclosed in Moola Bulla Station in 1955, when the government sold it to private buyers. And nearly forty years later, Geoff stood among the mourners waiting patiently for me to continue my tribute after ushering in the aircraft. I punched away at the walkie-talkie, according to the instructions Colin had given me and which I had scribbled on my program sheet and rehearsed successfully, twice!

126.35
118.60
KFI (Kilo Foxtrot India)
OCM (Oscar Charlie Mike)
URX (Uniform Romeo X-Ray)
Hit bottom TRANSMIT button.

Nothing! Try again. Nope. I looked around desperately for Colin. He was at the gate, greeting more mourners. I muttered an excuse to those nearest me and called to him. He took the walkie-talkie from me, tried to activate it, without success, uttered a mild expletive and took charge of the situation in a split second. He thrust the useless item into my hands. 'Keep em entertained! I'll drive over.' Keep them entertained? Agh! I'd almost shouted 'MAYDAY! MAYDAY!' into an unresponsive walkie-talkie. But I imagined some wag calling back, 'Yeah, we know the date, but so what? Get on with it!' Even with the nervous sweat filling my eyes, I could see the dust Colin's Falcon was kicking up as he screamed off to the airport, so I knew it wouldn't be long. But how long is a piece of string? How long is 'not long' when you've said all you wanted to say in a eulogy, used up all your prepared ad lib points, but all eyes are still on you, all ears waiting for you to introduce the fly-past? How long is it permissible to let people stand in the open sun, many of them dressed in suits and dark mourning colours? The words of an old gospel blues ran through my mind:

> *How long, oh please, how long Lord?*
> *How long 'fore I get to Heaven?*
> *Tell me, how long?'*

And for a moment, I envied Sandy, sealed up peacefully, out of the sun ... body and soul waiting to be sent on their separate journeys ...

That's it! 'Spirit country', he'd said. Our souls! And thus I slipped into my longest ad lib, ever. In radio, before computers took over studio operations, we all went through some hairy times, having to fill in time when a record wouldn't play, or there was a technical problem ... but there was usually some written advertising copy sitting on the desk and other programs we could talk about. And nobody could see us grimacing, or hear us shouting to the control room for help as we followed the sweep of the second hand on the clock, willing it to get to the top for the News to commence.

Frankly, I prattled. On and on, as coherently as I could manage, I prattled, and loudly, having no microphone and an open-air audience. I prattled nervously about how only that week my schoolteacher wife had been in Halls Creek for a lightning tour of the East Kimberley during the school vacation and how I had driven her up the Gibb River Road and out to Glenroy and Mt House Stations where her late father had spent all those seasons with Air Beef and her comment that she was certain that if there really is such a thing as a soul, or a spirit left after death, her father's would be there, hovering over the old cracked concrete airstrip where the Bristol freighters once took off with their loads of refrigerated beef carcasses ... Prattle prattle. I was squinting through the sweat towards the airport, praying for the sight of the Cessnas and praying that the police hadn't stopped Colin's car, which must have hit double the speed limit ...

Prattle prattle ... (Gasp! At last!)

'And as we are about to send Sandy Taylor off into the next life, we look across towards the airport we can see Paul and John approaching to ... '

The roar of the planes took over. Brilliant timing chaps! I had run out of words. Exhausted. Tears mixed with the nervous sweat. Tears of sadness, of course; tears of relief, too. My part was over. The planes dipped their wings in salute and turned for a second low sweep over our heads, before returning to base.

The coffin lowered into the ground ...

Rose petals sprinkled ...

Grave filled ...

I stood, calm now, reflecting on the friendship over the past nine months, shopping at Taylors' Store, chatting with Libby, enjoying a meal with the family in the amazing house that Sandy had renovated and extended, a haven from the heat, air-conditioned rooms, library and record shelves, dining table, paintings on the walls, a tour of Sandy's labyrinth of workshop, darkroom, storeroom containing a Link pilot trainer he'd bought years earlier in Sydney, for $2,500 and now worth about $30,000 on the collectors' market. And out the back, an old Suzuki two-stroke, four-wheel drive, awaiting restoration ... not by Sandy, but by one of his daughters, after she finishes school in Sydney. Another daughter paints. I've seen her work. She's good. A special family, the Taylors. We've lost a special bloke. I've lost a special friend.

Hugs and comfort for the family as the mourners dispersed. Colin had returned. He sidled over.

COLIN: Sorry about the buggered walkie-talkie. But nice one, mate. You did good.

ME: Me? It was you! How fast were you going by the time you passed the hotel?

COLIN: No idea. So, what did you say to fill in the time?

ME: No idea. I've gone blank. It might come back, one day.

It did come back, the very next day, which was the twenty-fourth anniversary of my father's death. I often think of friends and mentors who have gone. My father was both friend and mentor and so was Sandy Taylor. Some time after I'd written about Sandy's funeral in my diary, when I was approaching the end of my secondment, I wrote about my feelings for Halls Creek. New friends of both races, the surrounding landscape which I had been exploring during my free time, and the town itself – despite some problems I had encountered along the way: they had all got right into my bloodstream. I had been missing my family and friends back in Perth, of course, but these people and this place had changed me forever. It was the answer to my old question: *Am I there, yet?*

July, 1994: LAST DAYS AT YARLEYEL
You know it's got under your skin when you've been
up off the highway out of town,
a rough track, you've seen some conflict, you're
coming back
and it's dusk as you reach the top of the last
jump-up and there it is!
You catch your breath at the sight, the town lights in
the shallow valley,
greens fading into grey night, the 'oasis'. You round
some corners into your street,
your haven, and the word 'home' sings off the
tongue, so sweet.

HONG KONG TO FITZROY CROSSING: THE ROAD LESS TRAVELLED TO A FAMILIAR PLACE
DONNA BING-YING MAK 麥

冰

瑩

I was born in Hong Kong, the daughter and first child of parents whose families were originally from mainland China. Unlike traditional Chinese who wish to return to their ancestral lands after they die so that relatives will tend their grave, I want my ashes to be scattered into the Kimberley's Fitzroy River at Fitzroy Crossing. While Hong Kong (where I still have relatives) was my birthplace, and the village of Tiegong in Guangdong Province is my ancestral and biological home, the Fitzroy Valley is my spiritual home. This is the story of how I travelled from one family, place and culture to another, and how each has helped me to understand and appreciate the other.

Like many Southern Chinese diaspora, my paternal great-grandfather was a coolie or indentured labourer.

Unlike many coolies who died or never returned home, my great-grandfather saved enough money to return to China and marry more wives; his third wife was my paternal great-grandmother. My grandparents moved from China to Hong Kong around the time of the Second World War and the Japanese occupation of China. The son of my paternal grandparents, my father, was recruited for medical specialist training to the Colombo Plan in 1964–65, so he and my mother left Hong Kong for Melbourne where they stayed for one year, and then returned to Hong Kong. But in 1969, we emigrated to Perth, where I started school. Although I knew my ABCs and could add up two columns of numbers, courtesy of a Hong Kong kindergarten education that prioritised academic achievement over play, I spoke no English. Luckily for me, ESL (English as a Second Language) programs for migrant children didn't exist, so I learned English by immersion, and in three months was speaking fluent Strine.

After my mother's death, the seed that had been sown while I was a medical student in the Kimberley town of Derby, germinated. By taking a position as one of two doctors in Fitzroy Crossing, I entered another world and gained a new home. I recently found out from a doctor who was one of my supervisors, and is now a very dear colleague, that she doubted whether a private school girl would survive in Fitzroy Crossing. But instead of surviving, I thrived. Despite the physical, and probably because of the cultural differences between Fitzroy Crossing and Perth, it didn't take long for me to feel comfortable – more comfortable in many ways than I had felt in the city. And whilst I was aware that my position of privilege as a doctor must have influenced the way in which people behaved towards me, I felt accepted for just being me. This feeling has never left me; to the contrary, it seems to grow stronger each time I return to the Kimberley and especially when I go back to Fitzroy Crossing. My eleven years in the Kimberley, first in the Fitzroy Valley and then in Derby, 'grew me up', as its people would say, and shaped me as a person and a doctor, as much as my biological family.

Margie, an Aboriginal school teacher, took me on my first fishing trip, near the old river crossing. She taught my husband and I how to use a throw net to catch freshwater prawns, called cherrabun, and bait fish for catching barramundi. We often returned to this part of the river in the evening after work to catch cherrabun for dinner. In the wet season, after the tourist boat tours had finished, my husband would launch our eight-foot, bright orange bathtub of a boat into Geikie Gorge. We would sit on the rocks in the middle of the gorge for hours on end, fishing with live bait and keeping cool in the over forty degree heat by going for a swim every now and then. If we saw freshies (freshwater crocodiles) we would splash around a bit to scare them away before plunging in. Margie's brother, Ritchie, took us hunting with his friends Joy and Jimmy and some of their young family, including Delphine and Bronwyn, on Gogo Station. On the way to the hunting place we came across Ivan and his family in a river bed. Although he had a big mob of people with him, Ivan invited us to sit down for 'cuppotea' and shared some of their crocodile with us. Later we caught a goanna with eggs in its belly, and a wild duck. I'll never forget the rich buttery taste of those eggs cooked inside the goanna in the coals, or being taught by Delphine and Bronwyn how to pluck a duck without scalding the skin in hot water, cook it in a billycan and serve it up on a 'bush plate' of leaves and small branches pulled off a tree. Coming from a 'foodie' culture, I was eager to learn how to catch, prepare, cook and eat anything, and grateful to have so many willing and generous teachers.

One afternoon, a bunch of what the locals referred to as 'old women', including Daisy, Paji and Stumpy (who always called me 'bubby', whilst I was Dr Donna to everyone else), came by the hospital and asked me to go hunting with them. We travelled about half an hour along the highway towards Derby and soon after getting out of the car I was instructed to 'siddown under that tree with the old man' (Paji's husband, Boxer) while they went hunting as I wouldn't be able to keep up with them. I couldn't understand it at first, but I did later. The skill, agility and endurance of these women, old enough to be my grandmother, was amazing. In town they moved slowly like old ladies, and complained about aching knees and backs. Out bush they became hunting and gathering goddesses. When the women returned, they brought back a large-blue tongue lizard that they cooked in the coals. I was told to give the whole thing to Paji's old husband, and was left with an old, stringy bush potato to eat! Although I was a bit disappointed, I was not surprised as reverence for elders is also an important part of Chinese culture. As a child I had been admonished for not always showing respect.

I later went hunting with my husband and a medical student, shot a goanna (I had learnt how to shoot by then) and cooked it in the coals. I couldn't eat it all so I gave it to an old man whom I was looking after in hospital. He devoured the beast within seconds with great relish, and the look of joy on his face as he ate remains with me. A similar thing happened when I dropped by Boxer's house to give him a bush turkey. The importance of food and of sharing it with old people – especially highly-valued foods like goanna or bush turkey – was a very familiar practice to me.

When I heard elderly Aboriginal men and women being addressed as 'old man' and 'old woman' as a sign of respect, it brought back memories of how Chinese people address their elders with similar titles that literally mean 'old uncle' or 'old aunty'. It helped me appreciate how much age is valued in both these cultures, and highlighted their differences with the youth-obsessed West.

Language reveals a lot about the cultural values of those who speak it. Knowing your place within your family and how you fit in and behave towards other family members is very important to Chinese people. Our language doesn't have generic words like 'cousin', 'uncle' or 'aunty'. Instead, there are different words specifying each family member, and these tell us where that person fits in with everyone else. For example, when I address my 'aunty' using her correct title (in which her given name is an optional extra), it tells me her birth order in her family, whether she is my father's sister or my mother's sister, and whether she is younger or older than her sibling who is my parent. When we go out for a meal with extended family, it is the oldest family member who pays because they have obligations to care for those younger than themselves. In return, the younger ones must show respect and gratitude in their words and actions.

Chinese culture is centred on families and social groups rather than individuals. Even though I didn't consciously recognise this at the time, it may be one of the reasons that I easily accepted the concept of Aboriginal kinship and the skin system, and saw the advantages of working within it even though I didn't understand it fully. I remember Brenda, one of my patients, telling me that if I needed help to persuade 'Jane' to have a particular medical treatment, I should talk to her grandmother or aunty, not her mum. I was grateful and felt privileged to receive such advice from my patients and Aboriginal health-worker colleagues, and tried to incorporate their advice into my work as best I could.

My Chinese upbringing helped me in my work in other ways, even though I didn't appreciate it at the time. Looking back on my approach to patient care, I realise my early lessons in deference to authority meant that unlike other health staff I was not afraid to be assertive. I never asked patients if they 'would like to' have a certain examination, test or treatment, which was the done thing in polite Western culture. When you think about it, it's quite obvious that very few people 'like to' take their clothes off to be examined or have an injection. So I would talk straight the Chinese way: 'I need you to lie on the bed and take your shirt off.' Sometimes I'd stress that even though patients might not want to do what I requested, it was an important part of 'doing my job properly' – an idea my patients seemed to understand easily.

My 'straight talking', a liability in Perth, was valued in the Kimberley, not only by Aboriginal people but also by many non-Aboriginal people on stations. I found this out thanks to Joy, a community health nurse and kartiya station 'missus', who has lived in the Fitzroy Valley for more than thirty years and is one of my dearest friends and teachers. It's an incredibly liberating feeling to be able to say what you mean and not have to waste mental energy creating euphemisms. To be liked because of it was an added bonus. I was far more productive at work there than anywhere else – another reason why I feel so at home in the Kimberley.

Before I moved to Fitzroy Crossing I had never come across pastoralists or station people. My patients and colleagues taught me the importance of this industry and its people to the history and cultural identity of the Kimberley. My own culture, in which the work ethic is paramount and you are expected to cope with adversity not by complaining but by getting on with life and work, made it easier for me to understand station people and their reluctance to seek medical care until they were very, very sick. I admired their values, resourcefulness and 'can-do' culture that are far more aligned with Chinese values than a 'passive welfare' culture that, to me, seems to have done as much harm as good. Chinese society has always allowed upward mobility of its people through economic and educational attainment. This is the outward expression of a belief that people should be allowed to determine the life they want for themselves and their family. Despite her headmaster father, my paternal grandmother left school when she was around ten years old and was married at sixteen because that was what girls did at the time. She soon realised her husband was going to take additional wives whether she liked it or not; that was what men did. She had seen firsthand how this threatened a family's dynamics and dispersed its economic resources, and although only in her early twenties, she took control of the situation by finding her husband suitable co-wives whom she would be able to get along with. Unlike many Chinese households of the time in which each co-wife and her children were housed separately to prevent jealousy and arguments, my grandmother managed a household with her husband, three additional co-wives and fifteen children living under one roof – an impressive achievement in human-resource management and emotional intelligence.

Reciprocity, a value that I have learned is a fundamental part of Aboriginal culture, is equally important to Chinese people. As a child I remember my mother always taking a small gift for the host whenever we visited someone's house or were invited out for a meal. The concept of to-ing and fro-ing is central to any relationship, be it family, friends or business.

We left the Kimberley soon after our children started primary school because our backgrounds put formal education before the social advantages of growing up in a small community. It was important to us that our children were in a school where the majority of students attended most days and always strived for academic excellence. Although our children's future was our first priority, when we left I couldn't help feeling that I had received far more from the Kimberley and its people than I had given, or could ever give, in return. But then the colleague who in 1989 thought I wouldn't survive six months in Fitzroy Crossing recruited me fourteen years later to the new medical school that she was establishing. And she had a special request. One of the first things she asked me to do was to develop a program that would make our graduates want to work in rural and remote Australia. I knew from my own experience that to make it work we needed to do something that would not only teach students the medicine, but also how to live 'out bush', and that the only people qualified to teach them are the people who live there. For me, this was never just about educating medical students – it was about reciprocating. And giving ordinary Kimberley people the opportunity to shape their future doctors was the most valuable thing I could offer.

On my first visit back to Fitzroy Crossing with my students, I stopped near Bayulu, an Aboriginal community, to give two middle-aged men a fifteen-minute ride to town. They recognised me immediately despite my seventeen-year absence. One man said, 'Dr Donna, we know you! You're always welcome in this country.' In 2010, while I was visiting Laurie and his family, he said, 'Dr Donna, you know you've got a lot of family here.' I know that these are not polite, empty words because of the smiles, hugs, kisses and tears of joy with which I am always greeted, and because families unfortunate enough to have been allocated a rare 'dud' student continue to host students in subsequent years.

Recently, one of my medical students, who had grown up in northern China, reminded me of a Chinese value that has influenced my life in a very pervasive way. He told me that some students were speaking disrespectfully about me and other members of the academic staff. He wanted me to know that he felt upset when students spoke badly about us because he had been taught to 'honour your teacher as you would your mother and father'. By teaching me and caring for me, the Kimberley has taken on the same importance in my life as my biological family. When I take my students there it feels as if I am taking my children on a visit to their grandmother. The excitement and joy of the visit, of running the Kimberley program, doesn't come without feelings of great responsibility and anxiety. Each year I worry that students won't see the importance of showing proper respect to the Kimberley people who have volunteered, out of the goodness of their hearts and their regard for me, to share their lives and teach the joys and challenges of living 'out bush'. When I brief my students in preparation for the Kimberley, I say that when I take them to the Kimberley, I feel the same excitement and apprehension that they do when they take a serious boyfriend or girlfriend home to meet their mother and father. If they are really listening they know I am asking them to walk in the shoes of my ancestors by showing proper respect to the people of my spiritual home.

BREAK A LEG!
MARMINJIYA JOY NUGGETT

On a hot Sunday, Jimmy took Amy, my mum, as well as my mother's mother, granny Walka, on board a boat to the other side of the Fitzroy River where there was a lovely sandy area to have lunch and swim. Then he came back to pick up my mother's kartiya ngapurlu, Sandy, and me. Sally, my dog, didn't want to go on the boat. She had to swim behind us. After, Jimmy and me went off to do some fishing. All that morning we didn't have any luck with catching any parlka. We decided to go and have lunch with Amy, Sandy and Walka.

Jimmy and I told Sandy, Amy and jaja Walka that we were going to try some more fishing off the boat. As we got up and headed towards the boat I asked Sandy to say 'good luck' to us so we might be able to catch some barra. But she called out to us both, 'Have you heard of the saying "break a leg"?' Then I said, 'Yes, but isn't that the opposite of good luck?' Sandy called back, 'Yuwai, but if you say "good luck" you won't get anything. Try saying "break a leg" instead. That might bring you good luck!'

Jimmy manoeuvered the boat to a good place where

there were no logs or snags in the water that we knew would hold barramundi. As we threw our lines in the water, we both called out loud, 'Break a leg!' Two throws later, I had a strike! I was so happy after I caught my first barramundi. During all the time we had been at that part of the martuwarra before, we had missed nearly eight barra.

Late in the afternoon I caught another one. Jimmy had no luck but he did miss a few on that day. Since the time Sandy told us to say 'break a leg', Jimmy and I have always used that saying. We went back to the same spot many times and caught more and more parlka. Jimmy and I will always use the saying every time we go fishing. The reason we think it's special is because all the years we went fishing in that part of the river we had not caught one barra in our life.

JANDAMARRA IN TRANSLATION
STEVE HAWKE

Jandamarra is a legendary figure. He was once known as 'the black Ned Kelly'. As with Kelly, there are many versions and interpretations of his story; books that vary wildly in their accounts, numerous oral histories and stories, songs and dances. In 2008 a Fitzroy Crossing company, Bunuba Films, presented a stage version of the Jandamarra story at the Perth International Arts Festival in a co-production with the Black Swan State Theatre Company. The play script drew on many sources: it contained elements and incidents based on historical records, the odd line drawn from official accounts such as police reports and parliamentary debates, and insights from Howard Pedersen and Banjo Woorunmurra's book *Jandamarra and the Bunuba Resistance*. It also played with the known history – both the Aboriginal and the white versions – selecting, melding and blending characters and incidents. In its detail it was mostly pure invention, informed by knowledge of the sources and the time and place. It was a work of dramatic fiction with its roots in history.

As the writer, I tried above all to be true to the spirit of Jandamarra and his story as his people, the Bunuba, remember them. Over twelve years of writing, rewriting and polishing film scripts, and of creating and translating this version for the stage, I had at all times worked with Bunuba people. I take credit as the writer, but the copyright to my creation is owned by Bunuba Films. My rendering of the Jandamarra story belongs to them.

Jandamarra is a play about the frontier, set in the 1880s and 90s. It portrays four distinct linguistic worlds. There are the white pastoralists and police, speaking English to each other; and there are the Bunuba people, speaking the Bunuba language amongst themselves. Then there is the overlap between the two worlds. One is where Bunuba people and Whites talk to each other in pidgin English. The other is where Bunuba people talk to non–Bunuba speaking Aboriginal people in Kriol, which is a complex language in its own right, quite distinct from pidgin.

Writing the play in English, I was always aware of the inherent shortcomings and discrepancies when adapting the dialogue to the different linguistic situations. Quite apart from the challenges of language, there was the daunting matter of imagining myself into the daily lives and mindsets of nineteenth-century Bunuba people living a bush life. Despite the input from my Bunuba speaking colleagues over the years, there was always a degree of discomfort, an awareness that the fit would never be perfect; that words and concepts

I put in the mouths and minds of my Bunuba characters were unlikely to be entirely authentic.

And so we came to the first reading at the Black Swan Theatre's rehearsal room in Perth, in May 2006. Danny Marr and Selina Middleton had come down from Fitzroy Crossing to represent the Bunuba mob. We were a couple of actors short, and Danny read the part of Marralum – a fierce warrior initially antagonistic to Jandamarra – with aplomb. I can't remember which scene it was that provided the trigger during our discussions, but it was one set in the Bunuba world. All of a sudden there was this big, big conversation happening about the best way to do the scene. Without me quite realising, Tom Gutteridge and Zoe Atkinson from Black Swan were talking to Danny and Selina about doing the scene in Bunuba, and soon a consensus emerged that we should use Bunuba and Kriol in all the appropriate scenes.

I was momentarily stunned. I had always just assumed that it would not work to do Bunuba on stage. How on earth would the audience get it? But Tom assured us it could work using surtitles as occurs at the opera, and that it would enhance the play. At that moment my excitement and enthusiasm – already high – doubled.

Three months later I was sitting down in Fitzroy Crossing in the company of three amazing women, with a tape recorder plus a copy of the script with all the Bunuba elements marked in yellow and all the Kriol elements marked in blue. Mona Oscar is in her seventies; a woman of the station era, and a fluent

Bunuba speaker. Patsy Bedford, then in her fifties, works for the Kimberley Language Resource Centre; recording, teaching and promoting the Bunuba language is her great passion. Selina Middleton, in her forties, is one of the directors of Bunuba Films, and has often worked with Patsy on Bunuba language projects.

Over the course of three intense days we rendered the 'yellow bits' of the script into Bunuba on tape. It was an amazing experience for all of us. For me, as the fourth cog in the wheel, it was as intellectually challenging as anything I have done. I am no linguist, but I knew the two languages were completely different, not just in terms of structure, grammar and vocabulary, but more importantly, in terms of their complexities and the world views and attitudes that they have evolved to represent and depict. It was a line-by-line, phrase-by-phrase exercise, full of unexpected twists and turns. A three-line sentence of English dialogue could be precisely rendered in three Bunuba words laden with suffixes. Occasionally the reverse would apply; a perfect translation of a concise English phrase might require a much longer burst of Bunuba dialogue.

At times the limits of my cultural understanding were exposed. 'A mother can't talk to her son like that,' I would be told; and an alternative way of conveying the information or the dramatic point would have to be found. On a few occasions my analogies or verbal flights of fancy defeated us, and lines of dialogue would have to be dropped as unrealisable in Bunuba. But nothing intrinsic and, as writers so often find, on examination the script happily survives the loss of a gem they have laboured over. Time and again I would be delighted when the three women laboured and debated over a line, until one of them – usually Mona – produced a phrase, at which the other two would grin and say 'yes', then provide me with the 'back translation' from the Bunuba to English; and I would have a phrase more apt, more dramatic than my original.

I had written an exchange between Jandamarra and his mother Jinny, in which she is pleading with him to leave the white man's sheep station and return to the camp of the Bunuba living in the bush, free, but on the run.

'Men are born to be hunters, not the hunted,' he says.
'The Bunuba were born to be free in this land, not white men's slaves,' she throws back.
'I'm no white man's slave,' he declares.

Bunuba has no word for 'slave', no remotely matching concept. It was an amazing, and very stimulating hour, as we discussed this back and forth, until we came up with a completely different exchange, with alternative declarations and analogies that rang much truer.

On the fourth day Patsy and I made a start on getting some scenes down on paper in the Bunuba version. Sometime later, Mona's daughter June Oscar, who amongst her many responsibilities is the chair of the Kimberley Language Resource Centre, got to work with

Patsy, and then with me, on the full written version. June has a fine eye for detail, and the spellings and grammar were tweaked and refined, and the text analysed word by word. During this process it became apparent something else was happening. The act of rendering and then analysing the Bunuba was freeing June and the other women to contribute and comment on the content in a way they could never feel free or able to do with my English text. This was not just a matter of cultural niceties and protocols. We found ourselves engaged in a critical and dramaturgical discussion of the content, which was about ensuring a genuine portrayal of the Bunuba world and characters, whilst also serving the purposes of the drama.

I can't remember the last time I enjoyed myself so much. It was fantastic to see the thrill my Bunuba colleagues were getting out of working with their language in a written form at such a complex and demanding level. There was a sense that the Bunuba characters in the play were becoming true and were taking on a reality far greater than before. We felt we were venturing into new dramatic territory, where an Aboriginal language in all its complexity and richness would stand as a major, indeed an integral, part of a large-scale dramatic play on the Australian stage.

The translation process was only the beginning though. A play script is just words on paper. It only comes to life in the mouths of actors. Our Indigenous cast members included three Fitzroy Crossing men making their stage debuts, Kimberley stage veteran Ningali Lawford, and elder George Brooking as our singer; but the others came from across Australia. Four months before the play premiered they all spent two weeks in Fitzroy Crossing receiving intensive language training from June, Patsy and Mona.

Despite the doubts I harboured at times, it worked magnificently. June and Patsy stayed with the show throughout rehearsals and production as language coaches and cultural advisers. The show could not have happened without them. And, on opening night, a Perth audience heard Bunuba as a living and vital language.

Mona and Selina were amongst those who came down from Fitzroy Crossing for opening night. And in a sense, our most important critic that night was Mona. June said afterwards in an interview for the ABC's *Artists At Work* series, 'My mother said she cried. She said it was so true. She was very proud of the actors in telling the story so clearly ... It was a very proud moment for Bunuba people.'

By the time this collection is published, we will have achieved a dream of 'taking Jandamarra home'. In 2011 the play will tour four Kimberley venues. Most of the original cast will be with us for this new production, but we have a new director and design team, and the play has been dramatically reworked. We will be taking a different approach to the surtitles this time around. In Perth, the reality of operating the surtitles, and synchronising them with the speech of the actors on stage proved challenging at times. In some parts, there were simply too many surtitled words for the audience to read, whilst also taking in the action and emotion on stage. We have decided to reduce the English translations to a minimum to make it easier for audiences to follow. But the Bunuba language itself will remain as a central, essential component of the performance.

The highlight will be a season at Windjana Gorge in the heart of Bunuba country where many of the events in Jandamarra's brief life took place. The Bunuba people will hear their mother tongue in this extraordinary place, in the presence of an audience from across the world. It will be another proud moment. We hope that Jandamarra's spirit will be there too, watching and listening.

HOOKED ON HISTORY
CATHIE CLEMENT

In 1917, the cinema photographer William J. Jackson spent months filming on the Kimberley coast. Many of the local men were away at war but the Broome pearling fleet was still impressive enough to provide good footage. So were the scenes at scattered missions and the port of Wyndham, where a camel team, harnessed three-abreast, drew a cart piled high with eight tons of firewood. But the highlight of Jackson's 'Wild Nor-West' film, which thrilled Australian audiences before going to New Zealand and London in 1921, was his depiction of Aboriginal people hunting, fishing and engaging in ceremonies.

I first heard about Jackson's work in the late 1970s while completing an arts degree at Murdoch University. I had seen parts of the Kimberley while working in Derby in 1970, and, after reading anthropologist Michael Robinson's article about the film, I wondered what the region would have been like in and before 1917. That curiosity led to a research project and a realisation that, until at least 1920, Indigenous people in the North Kimberley had little contact with settlers. I was hooked. Here was a region where contact was not only comparatively recent but had evolved slowly and could perhaps be documented.

It was already known that commercial exploitation of Kimberley resources had begun in the mid-1860s when settlers took sheep to Camden Harbour and Lagrange Bay. Those people withdrew, defeated by the environment and Aboriginal resistance. A decade later, the northward expansion of the guano and pearling industries provided a platform for the renewal of exploration and settlement. Life was almost as hard for the second wave of pastoralists but, when thousands of prospectors flocked to Halls Creek in the East Kimberley in 1886, the trappings of 'civilisation' followed.

How difficult could it be to piece together an account of contact during the early settlement period? Historian Professor Geoffrey Bolton and author Dame Mary Durack had already written about stations established by small numbers of people in the major river valleys. Surely some of those people, as well as others who were passing through, would have written about instances of contact. Other people sitting in city offices would have recorded the allocation of land, the issue of licences, the movement of ships, and so on. The big question, of course, was how much the records would reveal about who was there, what they did, and how they interacted with one another.

A comment from Fred S. Brockman, who led a six-month survey expedition in the North Kimberley in 1901, suggested a cut-off point for an honours thesis:

> ... everywhere, even in the most inaccessible parts of the district, the natives all had iron implements, which had been roughly formed out of the iron tyres of vehicles that had been left far away from that part of the country during the goldfields rush, and which had been evidently passed on from one place to another.

Keen to discover how that situation had come about, I started recording everything I could find about people who were in the Kimberley prior to the end of the gold rush. I also documented maritime activities and mapped the early pastoral leases. Time got away, and only the pastoral leasing material, which was mostly about rhetoric and chicanery, went into the thesis.

Postgraduate enrolment afforded scope to continue the research, which soon became a consuming passion. Cryptic notes on index cards recorded thousands of individuals – Aboriginal, Asian, European, and a sprinkling of others. There were Americans pillaging guano, Australian and British-born pearlers forcibly recruiting Aboriginal labour, and New Zealand prospectors refusing to obey a quarantine order. The conflict typical of frontiers left its share of dead and wounded, while domestic violence claimed the life of Ellen Moher, the first non-Indigenous woman to live in the Fitzroy River Valley.

In the research, the interweaving of information from archives, manuscripts and printed sources highlighted discrepancies in various reminiscences. Some annotation and editing of those reminiscences followed, with Hesperian Press publishing G.H. Lamond's *Tales of the Overland – Queensland to Kimberley in 1885*. Its release in the centenary year of the gold rush was timely if coincidental.

As is often the case with mature-age students, changed circumstances called for suspension of my study. In the time out, I turned the data into what I called the Kimberley Historical Sources Project (KHSP). The project's aims were to continue the research and to publish the findings, topic by topic, in a series of directories. That grand plan eventually produced the *Kimberley District Pastoral Leasing Directory, 1881–1900* but, with no research funding available, the KHSP had to settle for spasmodic recording of data for eventual use in papers and books. The suspension of the postgraduate research left the way clear to participate in the Australian National University's East Kimberley Impact Assessment Project, which focused on people and country between Kununurra and Halls Creek. The KHSP data provided most of the detail for a paper on pre-settlement intrusion into the East Kimberley. It was, however, of little help when Eileen Bray (translator) and Helen Ross (editor) needed clarification of small points in the Aboriginal contributors' oral history. The answers to their questions lay hidden in numerous police patrol journals and other archives. So, another quest began and the answers went into historical notes, which were written about individual places to complement the oral history.

The months of immersion in the archives proved to be both rewarding and demoralising for me. The demoralisation came from repeated exposure to evidence of the abuse, brutality, and violence inherent in the imposition of a pastoral economy on Indigenous people's country. The rewards came from finding information that corroborated or clarified the oral history.

One unexpected reward highlighted the importance of accessing firsthand knowledge. The archival research had virtually ended but it had revealed nothing about two men – Roney and Markatiny – mentioned in the oral history. I had interviewed Maggie Lilly, a lifetime Kimberley resident, about Bow River Station and Turkey Creek but I had not thought to ask her about those men. Then, before saying goodbye, I asked out of curiosity if she had known Fred Terone. She had, and, after recalling his unusual laugh, she said that the Aboriginal people called him 'Roney' because they couldn't pronounce his name. There it was! Everything the archives had revealed about Fred Terone's character fitted 'Roney' perfectly. Unfortunately, Markatiny's identity remained a mystery.

By the time the impact assessment ended, I was acutely aware of never having seen Halls Creek, Wyndham, or any of the country in between. That changed in 1991 when a trip to Darwin afforded a chance to visit Wyndham. Seeing the familiar names of the creeks as the bus drove north from Kununurra felt like going home. Seeing Old Wyndham Port was wonderful. With little land available for development between the Bastion Range and the mudflats, and with most of the town's scattered development having taken place elsewhere, the locals had been able to preserve much of their heritage. It was intriguing to wander down O'Donnell Street – named after an early explorer and prospector – and see the port's history still evident in the street's collection of rustic buildings. The names associated with the small stores – Lee Tong, Gee Hong Yet, Fong Fan – hinted at the industry of the town's Chinese families. A much larger building on the other side of the street attested to the scale on which the firm of Connor, Doherty & Durack Limited had operated. There was much more to see but, like Halls Creek, those things had to await later visits.

Left to my own devices, I could have spent the rest of my life happily delving into the Kimberley of the 1880s and 1890s. But I needed to earn a living, and I had already resumed work on the doctorate on which I had embarked so long ago. The notes and index cards that had been consigned to the KHSP were no longer looking promising, however. The gaps in their coverage of early colonisation and contact were simply too big to be manageable. So, changing tack, I wrote a thesis about Kimberley exploration, land policy and land acquisition from 1644 to 1884.

Some of the gold rush and early contact material had

already gone into *Kimberley Scenes: Sagas of Australia's Last Frontier* that I coedited with Peter Bridge and published in 1991. Involvement in that project increased my awareness of the ramifications of unearthing historical information. To me, the people who had written the sagas were strangers from the 1880s. To their descendents, they were fathers or grandfathers, some remembered fondly, some not. The preparation of biographical notes about those men, undertaken where possible in consultation with their families, thus became much more than just research and writing. It showed very clearly that poking around in the past could have consequences in the present.

Working with the built environment proved to be less personal but soon showed that beliefs about local history are no less cherished than those about families. Research into the history of Derby's old police gaol, for instance, showed that, despite the stories on the bicentennial signage, the structure had no connection with Jandamarra, a Bunuba man who was also widely known as Pigeon. Long promoted as a local resistance fighter, he had been a prisoner in the original gaol at the other end of town.

Most of the Kimberley's heritage places have rich histories but those in Broome stand out because they also boast exotic elements. It was fascinating to research the history of the courthouse (originally a cable station), the bowling club (originally a ship-to-shore wireless station), Streeter's Jetty, Sun Pictures, and Chinatown. Other places such as the Derby woolshed and Wharfinger's House Museum, the former police buildings and post office in Old Fitzroy Crossing, the adjacent low level crossing, and the post office ruins at Old Halls Creek have less exciting histories. Yet, through their preservation, those places, too, show how various structures met people's needs in remote localities.

The built environment projects provided opportunities to work with skilled heritage practitioners who included Rosemary Rosario, John Taylor and Philip Griffiths. They also necessitated trips on which we met Kimberley residents, worked with them, and saw new places. But was it really work when Rosemary and I stayed at Birdwood Downs Station while we did Derby assessments, and then at Mornington Wilderness Camp while we assessed the Air Beef Abattoir and Aerodrome (ruins) and Glenroy Homestead Group? It was, but the same can't be said of spending the next night on Mt Elizabeth Station and enjoying an unexpected visit to the original homestead, which Frank Lacy and his wife Teresa had built in the 1940s.

Seeing a place for the first time is one of the most interesting aspects of pursuing Kimberley history. Places like the original Mt Elizabeth homestead are still so remote that one can only wonder at the drive and determination that brought them into being. More substantial homesteads, like those on Liveringa and Fossil Downs Stations, are closer to towns but are still testimony to the aspirations and stamina of those who built them and lived there. Other less heralded structures include Ivanhoe Crossing (out of

Kununurra) and Mary River Crossing (between Halls Creek and Fitzroy Crossing). Like the low level crossing at Fitzroy Crossing, those sturdy concrete roadways are permanent reminders of the ingenuity of government engineers and the energy of their construction teams.

Teasing out and testing the stories associated with places and people is both interesting and challenging. The Boab Prison Tree out of Derby might not have been used to hold prisoners but the Hillgrove Lockup – a hollow boab tree out of Wyndham – certainly was. Mounted police and trackers sometimes halted there with chained Aboriginal prisoners and witnesses. Some patrols enjoyed a smoko in the shade; others used the tree to hold their prisoners overnight before resuming the long and arduous trek to Wyndham.

Mobility and transience are very much a part of Kimberley history, and each place has its own stories. Those places include mines, airfields, and radar stations as well as others such as Bungarun (the former leprosarium, out of Derby), Moola Bulla Station (out of Halls Creek), Beagle Bay (north of Broome), Bidyadanga (formerly Lagrange Bay Mission, south of Broome), and Oombulgurri (formerly Forrest River Mission, out of Wyndham).

Mobility, transience, and fragmented records can make it difficult to determine whether pieces of historical information relate to a single individual but, when the pieces mesh, the result is really satisfying. One such instance occurred in native title research in which I put data into a long chronology that contained cross-references and phonetic analysis. Read alone, a sentence from Mary and Elizabeth Durack's book *Chunuma*, published in 1941, looked useful but not startling. Yet, in the chronology, their comment that a little girl named Dingyerri had come to Ivanhoe Station 'from the Keep' was invaluable. There, it bridged a gap between the past and the present by providing essential documentary evidence of a native title claimant's connection with her Keep River country (near the Northern Territory border). As children, Chunuma Rainyerri and Dingyerri had engaged in antics that provided the Durack sisters with stories for their illustrated books. As the children grew older, various people noted their presence but used inconsistent spellings for their names. Chunuma was recorded as Geoff Rungye and later as Jeff Djanama. In the 1970s, he told anthropologist Bruce Shaw about spending part of his childhood on Ivanhoe with his friend Sheba. That innocuous piece of information, combined with comments from *Chunuma* and archival records, showed that Djanama's fellow claimant had been recorded as Dingyerri and then as Sheeba Dilyarrie before she became known as Sheba Dignari.

At the other end of the scale is information that is found through nothing more than serendipity. The New Homes segment of *The West Australian* might seem an unlikely source for Kimberley history but, glancing at an article one day, I happened to notice some outback clothing in a photograph. The people in it were Kirsty and Damian Forshaw of Nita Downs Station. The article, as well as describing their new homestead, mentioned that fire had destroyed the old one. What a convenient way to discover the fate of a building.

In collecting such information, I can see a massive change in my attitude to the Kimberley and its history. At first, it seemed that only the earliest contact – something totally removed from anything that had happened in my lifetime – would be interesting enough to pursue. Yet, because the story of contact was interwoven with other stories, it soon became clear that each locality had its own interesting history. Few of those histories will ever be documented in detail but each would be intriguing to pursue. The same is true of the lives of many of the people who were there: people like 'Dutchy' Bening, who was among the so-called aliens interned during the First World War, and the 'Mountain Maid', who was one of the Kimberley's earliest prostitutes.

Had life taken a different turn, I might have been equally happy researching the history of another region or another era. But the pull of the Kimberley remains as strong as ever. That situation owes something to the formation of the Kimberley Society. Launched in 1994, it provides exposure not just to information about the region but also to people who have seen it from every conceivable angle. Some have worked in its industries, designed its bridges, built its roads, or provided its medical services. Others have studied its natural history, explored or exploited its natural resources, ventured into its many fabled gorges, or captured aspects of it in art, films or books. Chatting with such people, or listening to them present talks, adds depth to written history. Hearing research scientist Greg Keighery talk about the 167 species of weeds known to be in the region in 1999 was no less fascinating than hearing anthropologist Pat Vinnicombe talk about Aboriginal dance totems. In another memorable talk, David Welch, a rock-art enthusiast and researcher, demonstrated links between the Aboriginal people of today and the most ancient of the rock art by showing historical photographs of headdresses and other embellishments being worn during ceremonies.

Another important element of the talks presented to the Kimberley Society is that they save for posterity information that might not find its way into print elsewhere. One that comes to mind is 'Kinganna and Other Kimberley Coastal Settlements, 1920–1944', presented by anthropologist and archaeologist Ian Crawford. In another talk delivered soon after the Society formed, Noel Nannup, Western Australia's first Aboriginal ranger, told of being sent to Geikie Gorge in 1981 and being expected to deal, simultaneously, with conservation and tourism there and at Tunnel Creek, Windjana Gorge and Wolfe Creek Crater. In addition to the talks, the Society has held two seminars on rock art and one on history. Each seminar has given rise to edited proceedings.

On reflection, it seems that the setting of the Kimberley accounts for much of the diversity, vibrancy, uniqueness and complexity of its history. The remoteness, the rich resources, the striking landscape and the climate are all elements that make the region distinctive. Words cannot fully convey the bulbous brown boabs squatting on red pindan plains; long-legged jetties perched on mudflats; massive road trains taking cattle to port. Cameras can capture those things but, to really appreciate the Kimberley, you have to go there.

BY YOUR STUDENTS YOU'LL BE TAUGHT
ANDREW BURKE

Every morning in the dusty classroom, cooled by the shade of a big old gum, a small raggedy bunch of barefoot students and I would sing the school song. Whether there were two students or twelve, I would pull out the lyrics carefully written in black on a large yellow cardboard sheet and prop them up on the front table for all to sing. I would press play on the CD player and we would sing along:

> *Wanalirri story from the Dreamtime*
> *two boys 'em find kangaroo*
> *'em get 'im by the tail*

One morning I press the pause button and butt in:
 'Ha, that's a bit far-fetched, isn't it, kids ...'
 'Nah, mista, I catch 'em kangaroo one time ...'
 'Truly? They're very fast!'
 'We fast too! Me an Alan caught two dat time. We help Auntie put 'em on a fire ...'
 '... in a pit ...'

'Well, you truly surprise me, boys.'
'Lotsa things surprise you here, mista ...'
'... secret things, them old Mary tells ...'

then the rain came
they run inside the big Boab tree
it close up then they drown inside 'im
today you still can hear them crying

I break into the song again to bring it home to their daily lives and say, 'These days you can hear old men crying in the prison boab tree on the road between Derby and Broome. And tourist guides, too!' I laugh at my own joke. 'Stupid people have carved their names and the date when they were there into the tree, and littered the area so much, the authorities have erected a high wire fence around that tree to keep people out. It's so sad how some people can ruin things for others.'

Alan interrupts me, 'You show us one time, mista?'
'Sorry, kids, it's too far away.'
'Further'n Derby?'

Wanalirri story good for learning
Wanalirri school he good for me

One tree old man he got whiskers
Pull 'em he bring big wind and rain

Down by the old school – a corrugated iron shed that must have roasted students and nuns alike in the early days – stands a huge tree with a million nuts growing on it. Any spare daytime moment, the kids swarm over this tree, and this day, when we are out on a nature walk, they do the same There is no way of stopping them.

When at last I gain their attention, I ask, 'Why do you like climbing so high in the gulirri tree, children? If you fall you could break your neck —and some of those branches look very thin!'

'We get 'em nuts an eat 'em mista. You want some?'

'No way!' I laugh. 'They don't look edible. Won't they make you sick?'

'No!' The kids all laugh, slapping each other and pushing. 'Them good nuts!'

I stoop down and pick a few off the ground. 'Aren't these ones any good? They're certainly ripe …'

The kids all lean down and pick up a handful each.

'They only good for chuckin'!'

And the nut fight begins, the biggest nut fight of all time! Pretty soon I'm behind a tree trunk, taking cover. Even so, I can't help but smile at their happy faces.

and if you drive he'll tip the car and crash it
one time two people he bin drown
clap sticks play and chains they will rattle
today you still can hear them crying

It's the first funeral in the area that I attend. A young stockman from the community died when a ute rolled over on the way to Derby. I'm stunned by the anger coming from the pulpit.

'We are losing our young men needlessly,' the old high school headmaster says with passion. 'Just too many of our young men are dying like this – drinking and driving, speeding ...' He pauses, decades of frustration written over his face. He speaks from the pulpit as he has spoken to thousands of children as they have passed through his classrooms. 'How many times do I have to stand up here and say goodbye to another young man just beginning his life's journey? How many times do I have to ask you, beg you, to stop this carnage?' Anger gives his voice power and many are shamed as they sit in this chapel, their friend's coffin out front with his saddle on top. It too is going to the burying ground. Mr Jones stands up there, shaking with emotion. They don't look up. Now he is quoting numbers of the needlessly departed. Numbers. They know their friends' names. Now they hear an echo of old classroom days, Absent, absent, absent.

Oh Whiskers tree story good for learning
Wanalirri school he good for me.

My fellow teacher storms into the staffroom, sits down gruffly and folds her arms. 'I'm not going to that toilet until someone cleans it.'

'Why? Martha cleaned it last evening.'

'Yeah, well, the slimy frogs have jumped back in.'

I laugh, 'Don't let a couple of old tree frogs scare you!'

'I hate the slimy things.' She shivers. 'Just imagine them sticking their suckers on your bum!'

I push back my chair, put down my coffee and head for the toilets. Girls laugh as I walk in their toilet.

'Hey, mista, you girl?!' They giggle, 'You girl?'

I pause at the door. 'No, I'm on frog patrol, girls. Want to help me catch some?'

They all shrink back in horror, 'No way!' and shudder in disgust.

I take a deep breath and pull the top off four cisterns one by one. Little frogs, green as young leaves, cling on to whatever is handy. I pull them loose and throw them in a plastic bag. I flush one toilet, testing, and see the legs of more frogs clinging to the side of the rim in the rushing water. One by one I pluck them off, bowl after bowl, enjoying the game, the great white hunter in the pindan outback. Bag full, I leave the toilet and wave the bag at the squealing girls who run backwards across the dry grass. Archie, a helpful boy who plays basketball non-stop, is dribbling his ball down the verandah.

'Hey, Archie, do us a favour and take these frogs over to the well and throw them in, please ...'

I hardly finish when Archie shakes his head and runs backwards, surprisingly fast. So I walk on, across the dirt track and into the overgrown bush. Here an old well is home to frogs and snakes and wild lilies. Sinking down to my knees, I release the frogs out into the well. I mumble a goodbye: 'Good luck, you slimy buggers.' I stand and walk back just in time to see my fellow teacher hurrying off to the toilets. You gotta laugh, don't you, I laugh to myself, gotta laugh.

These are just two stories from Ngallagunda
Gibb River Station by the creek
Ngarinyin language spoken by the people
The old horse Nugget is gone but Ally's here

We need to tell our stories in the future
Tell 'em why the two boys are still crying

October, the entire school community travels to Broome in convoy: one big bus and a large four-wheel drive vehicle. A few mums and a handful of preschoolers, too. Broome has a community-based centre for visiting school camps, with spacious grounds, a football oval, swimming pool, games room and a hall. The convoy drives in and we unpack the bus, then rush to keep up with the children as they bolt for the best beds in the dormitories – girls one side, boys the other. Stars shine, wild shore wind whistles, full moon white-caps waves as they lap Broome's Cable Beach. The kids make wild claims of surfing prowess, and we simply smile, bushed after a day's packing, travelling and unpacking.

'We'll see how good you are tomorrow after a good sleep, hey, boys and girls.'

With tomorrow so far away, they find it difficult to settle into their strange bunks. We talk sternly but the moon is bright and their spirits are up, so it is hours before there is peace. All lie quiet in their bunks. Eventually the wind drops to a gentle hush. One young boy, ten or eleven, the artist of the school, gently intones:

'Good night, goanna,
'goodnight, snake,
'goodnight, bungarra,
'goodnight, kookaburra,
'goodnight, roo,
'goodnight, emu,
'goodnight, eagle,
'goodnight, hawk,
'goodnight, turtle,
'goodnight, stars,
'goodnight, sun,
'goodnight, moon.'

Silence. A young girl's voice pipes up from across the room's partition, 'Goodnight, world.'

Wanalirri story good for learning
The whiskers tree story good for me
Wanalirri story good for learning
Wanalirri School he good for me

DOUBLE VISION

STEVE GOME

It's the Dry Season. Somewhere out the back of Noonkanbah. A couple of Toyota Landcruisers packed full of people shudder down the road. Dust reaches into the sky like smoke. It's the whitefellas who call this time the Dry Season. The time of year when the sun gets stronger, the rivers dry up, and the old road across the riverbed at Fitzroy Crossing is used as a crossing and a diving platform. In the Dry Season, the water at the top of the river is warm. The swimmers seek out the pockets of cool water that lie beneath the surface current. When the whitefellas came up here, it didn't take them long to realise that the Kimberley is hot and dry country. The rain can come in only a couple of months in any year – or it might not come at all. The whitefellas discovered they became increasingly cranky in the weeks leading up to the time when the rain might fall. So they called this time the Dry Season and gave it some Capital Letters to show how much they were looking forward to the Wet Season. On this particular day in the Dry Season out the back of Noonkanbah, the mobs from Kurnangi and Gogo Station are going fishing. They have taken a couple of Toyotas, some nets and some lines. They have also taken along a kartiya family who have been living in Fitzroy for a few months. Although it was a long time ago, I remember that day very clearly. Every time I replay the scene in my mind, the frames are so distinct I can retrace the steps of each thought I had ...

I was sitting behind the driver of the second Toyota, looking out the window at the column of dust rising from the car in front. A kartiya boy; about ten years old. I had just started going to school in Fitzroy Crossing. The car was full of excited people laughing and speaking in a language that I couldn't understand. I was a little bit sleepy and I was daydreaming as I watched the shimmering haze around the spinifex. Through the window, the haze looked like a silvery halo. And then I would focus my eyes and see the spinifex that I knew – spiky and mean. Thinking about the spinifex in that way made my legs tingle with recognition. And so a game began. Relax the eyes; see the silver. Concentrate, see the spikes and feel the tingle.

The chain of Landcruisers came to a halt. Everybody was talking with excited voices and jabbering fingers. Kangaroo. Over there, see 'im. You see 'im?' Across the road, nestled amongst a cluster of shrubs, a kangaroo stood in the shade of a large tree. Bending, chewing, grazing. Unhurried. Over on the passenger side of the car, a big fella – well over six feet – with a curly black beard and sleepy eyes, rolled quietly out of his seat and stood in the middle of the road. He began crossing the road very slowly, shuffling purposefully. His clothes were earth-coloured, and they had the colours of the earth on them. A loose, faded shirt that may have once been green, and battered cords smudged with dust. Even in whitefella clothes, he looked like part of the landscape. This fella had a rifle by his side, casting a thin shadow on the red sand next to his solid one. All our eyes rested on his back. Would the kangaroo see him? What would he do next? The kangaroo pauses for a moment. Stops eating. Lifts up its head and looks around. It sees the hunter coming towards him. And the big fella keeps looking at the kangaroo. He keeps moving. Like a shadow, keeps moving closer.

As I watch, my mind is racing: What is happening? I don't understand, there's something wrong. Why doesn't the kangaroo run away? I don't think I'd ever seen a rifle before. I know I'd never been hunting. Apart from flies and mosquitoes, I'd never seen anything killed. And I knew that I was about to see the kangaroo die. But that was not what was unsettling me. The kangaroo is tame, I thought, maybe he was somebody's pet. This isn't hunting. An image from a tin of shortbread, of men in red coats on horseback and packs of baying hounds, appears in my mind. I am angry, wanting to yell at the hunter: The kangaroo doesn't have a chance if you get so close. You're supposed to give it a chance to get away.

Now the hunter is standing at the base of the tree. Out in the bush. They are still looking at each other. It looks to me as though he strokes the kangaroo's shoulder with the back of his hand. The rifle comes up slowly, and the kangaroo falls to the ground. And suddenly, it all gets incredibly noisy. Shrieks of excitement, laughter and congratulations greet the hunter as he returns to the car. He carries the kangaroo over his shoulder. When the kangaroo is placed in the back of the Landcruiser, I notice its blood smeared against its skin, and how the blood causes patches of fur to clump together. The vehicles start up again, and we continue out along the road towards the fishing spot. I go back to looking out the window.

I remember lots of talk about the kangaroo and the hunter. I overheard people in the car chattering about what had just happened – maybe in the Walmajarri and Kriol languages first, and then in English. I'm sure that night, as the day was being digested around the campfire, people were still talking about the kangaroo. And I was listening, ticking things over, letting things mingle with private thoughts.

Three decades have passed since that day out the back of Noonkanbah. But the memory of it remains strong. The memory of watching an Aboriginal man hunting a kangaroo in the bush, and having images of beagles chasing foxes flash through my mind. Of having no experience of hunting, but a clear sense of what proper hunting was.

I can't be certain that it was the big fella who I heard speaking in the car – or even that I heard everything that was said, but it's his face that I see when I hear the voice explaining: 'I was singin' to the kangaroo spirit. Tellin' him who I am. Where I bin come from. I was sayin' thank you for giving me his life.'

A PAIR OF FEET
LUISA MITCHELL

My mum loves the Kimberley. She loves Australia, but the Kimberley is the best, she says. I haven't made my mind up yet. I like the cities because I feel like everyone is one, always moving on and on, and when I think of that I feel good inside. But I love it here as well, because everyone knows everyone, we're all connected, all family. Maybe when I'm older I'll know where I belong, but for now I can't make up my mind.

The street I live on is really quiet. You barely see any cars on our road, although sometimes at night you hear the screeching of tyres as some crazy person deliberately makes skid marks all over the bitumen. I wonder why people do that ... there doesn't seem any real point to it.

It doesn't make any sense why our street is so silent, whether in the day or night-time. I tell you why? Because all the streets around us are so rowdy: dodgy, busy, or all three at the same time. It's like time comes to a stop when it reaches my street, and everything becomes so slow you can hear the wind moving through the mango trees.

I live with my mum and my sister. We're like a big

house of girls. I'm glad there are no boys in our house, or else we'd all have to be real secretive and not talk about girl stuff like we usually do. Mum says after I was born she had another boy, called Billy. I like that name. But Billy was already dead when he was born ... I should feel sad about it, but I don't. I just think, 'That's life. Sometimes we live, other times we die.'

Only mum and sister Lily remember Dad, and I'm really glad I don't. Lily said he was a mean old man, always grumpy and telling mum what to do. I can't imagine anyone telling mum what to do – she's her own boss! She certainly acts like it when telling me to feed the dogs.

I like going to school, but Lily hates it. She only goes if she's bored, but that's pretty rare. Mum doesn't push her or anything, because she thinks school's a waste of time. I reckon it's because she never went to school when she was a kid, that's what I think. I like school because I have friends there, and because I get to see Rezza Denkins every day.

Rezza's my boy, he said so. He says he loves no one else in the world but me, but I'm not sure because I saw him flirting with Tilly Newton the other day, and that made me real mad. When Lily's friend told Lily about my tomato-red face Lily wished she'd been at school for the first time in her life just so she could've seen my face. I was real upset about that, but I forgave Rezza anyway. He's my boy, you see.

There's a park at the end of my street, and it's not a very good park when you compare it to other parks. But

I love it. I love it because I've been going there ever since I was as young as six, so you see I've been living here for most of my life. The park used to have an old, graffiti-covered playground, but only when it was pulled out did I realise how much I missed it. Now the only thing left is a set of swings, and they aren't much fun.

My mum took me – not Lily! – for a drive out to Derby the other day, to the Birdwood Downs Station. I like that station because they have heaps of horses there, and I absolutely love horses. Mum only goes there to take photos of the bush – she's one of those hippy mums that have travelled around Australia with only a camera. There's one in every town, and this one isn't an exception. She likes the turkey bushes the best, because of their purple flowers. I prefer the black cockatoos, with their crazy hairstyles. They make me laugh every time.

My dream is one day to become a horseriding teacher, so I can teach kids all over the Kimberley how to ride horses. But you see, my school doesn't teach horseriding, so I have to have a 'smart' job, as Lily explained to me. I think I will become an author, because I love writing stories. Miss Elle said that I was the best writer in all of her English classes, and that's not much because there's only two, but I was really proud.

I was thinking about feet the other day. My friend Macy has little pink feet, all soft and pretty, and at first I was jealous because my feet are all big and dirty, and my toes stick out everywhere. But then the other day it was absolutely boiling, and we had sport. Everyone just wanted to lie down in the undercover area, but we had no hope. See, Mr Truppis is a cruel, mean old bull and he made us play soccer on the oval, no shoes and all! 'Course, I didn't care about the no shoes part. I barely ever wear shoes, and so my feet are so tough I don't feel the pain at all. But Macy, she sure did! She was hopping and squealing, looking for shade desperately, and I tried not to laugh but it was really funny. Now I don't care that my toes are all long and ugly, because at least they're super tough, not like Macy's silly little pink feet.

I've decided that I would rather live in the Kimberley than in the city. I love just sitting outside, listening to the sounds of the birds rather than the honks of the buses and cars that roam the city streets. Or maybe I've decided because there's a wonderful little park at the end of my street, with pindan wattles and medicine trees. That's certainly something to think of.

One of the main reasons is because if I had grown up in the city, I wouldn't have been able to go out to Birdwood Downs and ride the beautiful horses there, or see my little – actually quite huge – black cockatoos! The horses in Perth are probably all neat and tidy and don't bite at all. That may sound nice but it would be a bit dull, if you ask me.

Looking over all of it, though, the main reason stands out a thousand miles, as Miss Elle said once. It's the *feet* I care about. Imagine me, living in the city with tiny pink feet! I don't think so. Give me good old Kimberley over Perth any day.

LYRICS, POETRY, AND A PLAY-FUL EXTRACT

NORTHERN TOWN

JIMMY CHI

CFGDEmAm
(Chord progression)

Verse 1
There's a broken man
In a northern town
Who's wonderin' who will
Shout the next round
And through the seasons
He's always there
Waitin' thirsty,
For another beer

Verse 2
He don't care about women
He don't care about men
He don't care about children
He don't care about friend
His lifelong purpose,

Whether here or there
Is to keep on drinkin'
Lots and lots of beer

Verse 3

Now you may ask me
Who this song's about
Is it your friends here
Who never shout
Well the answer's simple
Oh so plain to see
Just line up those coldies
for my mates and me

Chorus:

And the seasons come
And the seasons go
And all eight seasons
Just ebb and flow
In his heart he knows that
He must exceed
Lots more drinkin'
than he ever needs

In his heart he knows that
He must exceed
Lots more drinkin'
than he ever needs

THE RIDE OF HIS LIFE
RICHARD DAVIS

you tokin too much
for ride that purluman
you pikimap lilbit
so lisin now

see that big fella
holed up in the chute
cheeky bugger, that one
a real demon detective
flank-strapped belly broadens to the earth
with killer vertical lift-offs inside
runway horns bear a flick and a gore
and hoofs are haters, bonecrushers, marrow-seekers

when you sit on 'im
'e can jump up
twist and curl
all ballerina and hammer
you can't breathe, your body slam so hard
and no Cuban heel, chap-leg

John Wayne costume gonna help you then
my boy

hey, that loudspeaker bin call your name
your number's up
an' just remember
you live, you jaunt and swagger
you fall, you just the groans of a crowd

VARIATIONS ON COUNTRY
C. ANN HOBSON

You imagine crocs, snakes, kites
circling, stingrays in the bay,
geckos under eaves and palms,
imported; boabs, elegant,
odd; neon bougainvillea.
You anticipate heat, light, glare,
contrasting green and pindan.
Mostly, you're saturated
by sound: a cacophony of
corellas, red-tailed black
cockatoos publicising
the latest place for a feed,
crows in the paperbarks, quiet
only in the drifting noon.
And voices, always, voices –
at top volume. Querulous, loving,
reprimanding, singing; country driving
deep blues, hip-jerking
arm-swinging beats and tunes
smothering the loss of songlines.

A fugue of scrapping, yapping dogs
reaches dissonant crescendo.
Across the street,
hip-hop bursts like a hydrant
from a parked car.
Two houses down,
Elvis, comeback sixty-eight
ushers in tonight's intermission.

BUTCHERMAN
ROBYN WELLS

butcherman
stands
behind the counter
feet firm
quick flip of the wrist
knife slices easy
through any kind of meat

butcherpaper
turned, folded
handed over
to the old blackfella
unsteady in line

a slurry of words
fall out
he shouts
and curses

his neat
butcherpaper
packaged meat

butcherman
dances the old man
to the flywire door
he falls
blood smears red
on a white tile floor

I order half a dozen chops
rib bones
and a steak–lean
butcherpaper
turned, folded
handed over

butcher savage
wipes his butcher's knife
and shakes his head
dead weary
I always give him a bit extra
when he comes in ...

outside
high-flying black kite
spies old countryman
in the street

neat
butcherpaper
packaged meat
turned, folded
handed over

DUGONG CONNECTIONS
KELVIN GARLETT

I am an Aboriginal person and a cultural man. I first met my friend from the Kimberley in prison. I was interested in fishing and we used to walk every day around the compound. He told me about his country. He had married a Noongar woman, so he had some Noongar relatives. He was a leader and custodian of his country, an expert in his knowledge of the tides and the sea. He was a pearl diver when he was young and lived off the sea. I said I would like to go to his place and meet his mob, and he said he would take me around the river and creeks in a boat. He explained the different types of fish and animals they hunted; what bait they used and which areas to go to. He talked about the dangers of saltwater crocs. I said I used a net to fish in my Noongar country along the Swan River and in the sea. We shared stories about family, and culture, and fishing. We used to tell stories to each other. We used to tell stories about when we'd go hunting with family, how we hand our knowledge and skills to the young people, and that the stars in the sky are where our spirits return. We have to go with other elders when in their country. If we go by ourselves we show no respect and sometimes bad things can happen, like people drowning, or dying in the desert. We have to be given permission to walk on their land. When I came out of prison he met my sons as well as my brother and said we were welcome in his country so we have a great friendship. One story I kept in my mind was about hunting dugongs. I wrote down what he told me, part of the story told to a child. It is also a story I want to respectfully share.

The golden moonlight shone on the dark sapphire
sea that night.
They headed out into the bay.
Restless waves gently rocked the boat eager to push
them out to sea.
As they looked up they saw a thousand shining
stars.
My people were watching over me
On that hot and still night.

'Don't you go to sleep my child
Or you won't see the dugong tonight.'
Keep looking at the dugong dreaming,
we got to hold on to our sea and land.
'We'll walk into the future.
We will walk hand in hand.'

Nostrils flaring; swallowing precious oxygen.
Diving down then coming up.
The dugong sprayed silver mist into the air.

They saw it on the horizon!
Dugong diving feeding time.
The engines were cut, 'Now quietly!'

'Don't you make no sound my child or we won't
see the dugong tonight!'
Tired eyes closing now; the struggle is over, sleep
has come.
Noises, shouting, laughing; rocking the boat and
the smell of smoke.
Small hands touch the huge velvety beast from the
sea.
'Daddy you got a dugong?'
'Yes my son ... I told you don't go to sleep or you
won't see the dugong tonight.'

A BACKDROP BLACK
LEON HENRY

Pitch white and tossed against
A backdrop black, exposing
Birds in flighty circumstance
To a storm from the north

Like white gums against
Amber hills steeped by erosion:
Cockatoos compete for canvas
In pictures so imposing.

FROM *ESCAPADIA*
PETER BIBBY

Scene 1: the road to Oombulu, red dirt through savannah, no towns.

Sheba and Tomco are driving in a ute loaded with swags etc. Sheba would not get a ride without Tomco because she's underfunded. They work in the same cause but different fields, his is Law and Culture, hers Human Relations, patch-up mostly. A social worker, she is keen on her culture and records stories as a sideline, maybe will make a book one day. The old men call her that ''pology fella' partly as a joke; they would really not like to address what her visit is about – domestic violence. Tomco was mission-raised by scholars; Sheba's been to university. They are friends drawn steadily closer; she twenty-eight and single, he forty-two and long married.

Sheba   I know you can't do anything about the condition of this unsurfaced obstacle course, but could you hit the bumps less hard?

Tomco	I'm trying to jump over them. Some corrugation so big they have valleys, it's better to stay on the tops!
Sheba	I didn't book an air trip.
Tomco	Dead ends are always rough. When you get there on this road, that iss the end, nowherc clse to go, you got where you're going, and only come back with same bottom massage!
Sheba	So what do you hope to achieve, by your bottom massage?
Tomco	A signature and safe return.
Sheba	Well steer straight. Nothing else?
Tomco	You calling for my dreams?
Sheba	Why not?
Tomco	It's bad luck to say. I already got my fingers crossed. I just hope I can leave a meeting without having to reach the decision outside, at fifteen paces, with star-pickets. Traditional way to settle grievances has its downside.
Sheba	What's the up?

Tomco	No jails. No legal jungle. No court costs and no perpetual criminals. The community deals with the offender in their own way and it's over, finished. He's free to get his life back together.
Sheba	After recovery.
Tomco	It might hurt, but he knows what it's for, punishment doesn't take years. In a Western system, you have forgotten what you did by the time it come to judgement, let alone the punish part!
Sheba	Well it's designed to remind you what you did, maybe to a woman with her arm still in plaster.
Tomco	I fought for traditional law to be recognised, when it was just laughed at, but now, it has a place ...
Sheba	For women and kids I hope, no more swollen eye and cotton wool of silence covering up what someone is doing ...
Tomco	Here's to your workshops. And what else you want?
Sheba	Like you, I don't want to say what more ...
Tomco	You superstitious too?

Sheba	No, just don't want to be laughed at, like you. My dearest wish ... is just a silly ambition really, incongruous for me, being a mediator, I mean my speciality is conflict resolution ... but I want to take home something that speaks for this country of tall grass and taller anthills ... a spear, a real traditional spear, a big one.
Tomco	What you want a thing like that for?
Sheba	I'm fascinated by tools.
Tomco	You a collector!
Sheba	Why are you looking like that? I do have a collection, of implements. The oldest is a flake of stone that was a knife who knows when? I love those filleted edges, still sharp after ages, the way they come into your fingers and fit, exactly as they were held by the hand that made them ...
Tomco	When your home is a museum, your life is a collection.
Sheba	There's still something missing.
Tomco	Plenty of people in that condition. Put on the music.
Sheba	Do we really have to listen to Patsy Kline again?
Tomco	It's the only tape.

Sheba	One tape for eight hundred kilometres!
Tomco	Well you left all my other singers-to-riot-for behind.
Sheba	I left? You left. Who packed the car?
Tomco	Well it's my vehicle sort of but you should have checked. I wonder what the next disaster will be. Never one without two; never two without three.
Sheba	Don't call Patsy Kline a disaster, just an oversight, your oversight, and overkill by the eighth hour of hearing straight. What are you doing?
Tomco	Reading the submission.
Sheba	No you're not. Watch the road.
Tomco	You watch the road, if you're so worried about it. I'm worried about the submission. Where's my glasses?

He is groping along the dashboard.

Sheba	Tomco, you can't read and drive!
Tomco	Not without my glasses ... they in the glovebox?
Sheba	No. Anyway, it's too late to change the submission, it's gone in.

Tomco	Down between the seats?
Sheba	No. So there's no point worrying about whether you are a funded coordinator or tacky token. The decision is out of your hands.
Tomco	You haven't looked.
Sheba	I'm looking. Watch the road. The bloody road kills. A decision can only disappoint.
Tomco	And cost my job.
Sheba	Well that would be a picnic compared to waking up by the roadside with your neck broke, if you did wake up. Watch the road, please.
Tomco	Bloody wandering glasses.
Sheba	They're not between the seats! Or down the crack. Or on the floor. What about your pockets?

Tomco lets go the wheel and starts searching his pockets.

Sheba	Jesus don't you look, I'll do the looking – the wheel! Are you suicidal?

Tomco	Not that I know of, anyway I've been told I'll die by water. I like you feeling my pockets. I better lose my specs more often.
Sheba	I don't think even you could manage that, Tomco.
Tomco	What about right side? Any joy?
Sheba	Nope. Not in your pants pocket.
Tomco	I put 'em down, and I can hear myself thinking, that's where they are, but that little thought thinks my glasses are taken care of so then I forget them and then I can't find them.
Sheba	So then what do you do?
Tomco	Well if I don't think about it then I remember.

Suddenly his eyes widen and he slams on the brakes.

Sheba	Whatnow?

Tomco	I've remembered. The tree where we stopped to refuel in the shade! And look at English Gap. You wanted to take a photo.
Sheba	Now blame the photo for losing your glasses.
Tomco	I took them off to look at the view ...
Sheba	They were fogged up ...
Tomco	No, I have long vision. I put them down – on the dirt!
Sheba	We can't go back! It's a hundred kilometres.

He's turning the car around.

Sheba	That's three hours of supplementary travel. Fuel budget! We'll never find the tree – they won't be there.

Scene 2: Mango trees, inky black shade, remote community Oombulu.

Under the mango trees Aloysius and Vincible are both naked, sitting on sagging, rusting shearers' beds with an ash-heap between them. We don't realise they are naked until they stand, later. This is them, their protest and their way. Old is good. Very old is even better. Leaning against a fork of a mango tree is a bundle of spears, now weathered, bowed and useless, but fine as a bundle. In the tree is a worn .22 rifle with its stock wired together. Also in the treeforks: some clothes and ancient army knapsack, rope, wire, a derelict radio, spare billycans, etc.

Aloysius   Ute coming. No, ute going back.

Vincible   Can't make up mind!

Aloysius   It's that 'pology fella.

Vincible   Oooh, honeypot woman.

Aloysius   And that Cultureman coming to ask community about dancing.

Vincible   But coming or going?

Aloysius looks into distance.

Aloysius   He's looking for his eyes.

Emmi Sugarbush enters with a bucket of stew.

Emmi   You two put your clothes on.

Vincible   I got smoke to cover me. Poke the fire up.

Aloysius   But get the damper out first. I don't want my toast burnt.

Emmi   *(Planting the stew in front of the two men.)* Your granddaughter, Marianne, hopes you forgive her for blowing your grocery money on card game an' start talking to her again.

Aloysius   *(Plunging a mug in the stew.)* I forgive her that, but not leaving school and get pregnant.

Emmi   Marianne made the stew.

Aloysius   *(Hesitates only a second with mug and spoon.)* Good, we expecting visitors. According to my left shoulder bone.

Vincible   That the one the horse broke?

Emmi removes a damper from the ashes and knocks it clean on the ashes shovel.

Aloysius   That the one the horse didn't break, got the other side one, and right leg. Emmi, you got some of that hot cream for joint pain? Plaster me thickly and don't spare the squeezes.

Emmi   Go on, you old goat, you aging disgracefully, get your trousers on.

Aloysius   I'd rather stay how I was born. In the smoke.

He gets up and goes to the tree turning his back on Emmi, who is scandalised.

Emmi   Oh, shame, what cheek you got, and double.

Aloysius   That's my heart. No shame of myself. Like you of yourself, Emmi Sugarbush. You are true Escapadian.

Emmi   We all little Eskis now with our hearts in a coolbox.

Vincible	Before we just call 'im 'country' but in langwas 'Amboolgumin'.
Emmi	Langwas Centre says that's just the name *of* our langwas.
Aloysius	An' that's my country name. Whose borders is made of words.

Aloysius pulls a length of wood, actually a long root, from the stack in the tree fork and proceeds to clean the bark off it.

Emmi	Long time since you did that, old man.
Aloysius	Still haven't forgotten how.
Vincible	What you making a 'pear for?
Aloysius	Maybe I sellem at art auction in Shidney, *(grimly)* after I use 'em, make 'em real, what you say, Ricky ding dong Duggan?

As if by intimations, Ricky the Arts Project Officer comes on, bemused that he was announced before appearing.

Ricky	What are you calling me that for?

Aloysius	Cos you always have argument. I don't think you sleep at night, you don't get in bed you get in battle, but not with womans. With yourself! Hassen't met you match yet.
Ricky	I am fighting for you, so you don't get ripped off.
Aloysius	That's good but I hear you hate art gallery.
Ricky	I hate 'em and I love 'em. I love 'em when they sell you and I hate 'em when I think about it.
Vincible	Why? Art gallery paying us.
Ricky	They turn forty thousand years into a commodity. Tradition into disposable asset. Once that happens you lose ownership – of your soul.
Aloysius	Hahaha – you the new preacher. Art man preacher.

Ricky   Your store of generations is being raided
           and traded. Next thing they'll be putting
           you on Escapadian Stock Exchange
           and quoting share price for Oombulu
           Incorporated, you just an ethnic output!

Vincible   Share the price pretty good I reckon,
           long as it's a fair split. When they gonna
           do that?

Ricky   Never voluntarily. That's not the share
           you understand. Share market is divorce
           from responsibility. It's a financial fish
           farm in a feeding frenzy. Bottom feeders
           and big-gob top feeders. That's why I
           fight. I am fighting greed and selfish-
           ness ...

They are staring at him, part in admiration, part in disbelief.

Ricky   Emmi, I have a buyer for the waterhole.

Emmi   Oooh, that big one I did ... how much?

Ricky   You want me to give you the sit-down
           price?

Emmi   (*Laughing.*) What, you think I'm an old
           lady?

Ricky	No, you the girl star in career terms. But sit before you listen to this.

She remains standing, just hooks up her chin at him.

Ricky	Two hundred thousand.

Emmi	Hmm. *(She does sit, hollow voiced.)* That make me first grade?

Ricky	A-list. Top first grade. They sticking you in a New York office, if you agree.

Emmi	Hmm. Hmm. Lot of humbug from my nephew is accurate forecast. And suddenly lots of relation discovering me!

Ricky	Good. I want you to refuse. Then we can have a solo show – *(knows it is big ask, says it quickly)* if you do ten more paintings to put with your last-year crop. No pressure, but I have to set a date. We can get a good place in two months time. I don't want you to get exhausted, or do things in a rush, or for me, it's just, if you can, when you go solo, that's when you're a real artist.

Emmi	What's 'real'?

Ricky	Well ... people write articles about you, they spread your name, that's the thing, you can ignore what they say about the adherent beauty of your topicless meta-paintings, and the tonal interplay of your colours, and the arresting run of your lines. What matters is worldwide interest, you get 'stablished, it's different from being on a drip.
Emmi	I don't feel any different.
Ricky	You wait and see. It will pick you up, like a helicopter flying you to country, to paint for the camera. It will give you a funny feeling that you are someone else all the time and you will see other places than your own, big city that does all this to us, and supposedly for us.
Emmi	What about these old men, they artist, they going solo?
Vincible	We'll sit down. *(They do.)*
Ricky	This is not for everyone.
Emmi	They going into New York office?

Ricky	No, these men are B-list maybe, Buffalo maybe. Or a tower in Osaka, if I can squeeze 'em into Tokyo art show.
Vincible	Hah, we bottom rank, bare bottom rank.
Ricky	Not to me. That's what I hate about art market, more fashion than passion, like a choosy woman ...
Emmi	Choosy to me?
Ricky	While you are in flavour. Your name is high, Emmi Sugarbush, because of your colouristic tension. I can sell any half decent work with your name on it for six figures but all the time I'm thinking, is this bubble about to burst?
Aloysius	Make me a bubble.
Ricky	Too much narrative, uncle. You got to press into territories of abstraction. But don't listen to me. You want more canvas? More acrylics? Some new colour tubes and pots just arrived.

Aloysius	Everything, everything you got is welcome, as long as it don't mean you asking me next when am I going to use it! Cos I am busy making a 'pear for someone.
Ricky	Who? Not that art plane lady flying gallery owners around pretending just to be collectors and undercutting our exhibitions?
Aloysius	No this one is personal output.
Ricky	Who for? I've got to know, if it's for sale it's a product, it goes in the book.
Aloysius	I tol' you, it's for someone. Gift.

They exit, leaving Aloysius making the spear. He stops and pays attention to the action but without looking at it, as if his shoulder blade were the sense organ.

Scene 3: English Gap.

The ute is parked. Sheba comes walking towards it, having stopped searching. Then Tomco, bent over, studying the ground in a way that tells you he can't see it too well.

Sheba   Well here's the pass to glory but no glasses.

Tomco   Wait, a toolbit.

Sheba   What? Till you feel up the landscape? We've been over this ground. I'm not sitting here, I'll take another photo.

Tomco   Don't do that! You're appropriating the view.

Sheba   Or giving it respect.

Tomco   You think country needs your tiny respect?

Sheba   Sure do.

Tomco   You ain't even asked it first.

She's already clicking with the camera pointed at him.

Sheba   Stop!

Tomco stops with his heel on ground and toe raised. He lifts his foot and stoops.

Tomco	There, sitting perched on the winning-row, taking long view for their owner! 'Where have you been all this time, I knew you'd come back,' say my clarities, my fabulous focussers. My midlife revelations for eyes. Uncrushed.
Sheba	We can stop counting disasters.
Tomco	No we can't. The car is rolling!
Sheba	Funny how it sets off slow so you can't tell it's moving.
Tomco	Brake brake!

Sheba sprints for the car. It is very slowly, but irresistibly rolling.

Sheba	What can I do?
Tomco	Get in and put the brake on. (*He is dragging up a log.*)
Sheba	But it's going over the edge. I'm not getting in.
Tomco	It's a new car!

They are moving with it now. He's trying to match pace with the log.

Sheba	With all our gear – my wineglasses!
Tomco	(*Struggling with log.*) Get in. You think this is destiny; you want me to put this in the audit?

Sheba	You get in.

Tomco rams the log under the back wheels just in time.

Sheba	If you count near misses that was definitely horror number two.
Tomco	Backwards over English Gap – I could never explain it to the Canborrow mob. Inescusible loss of corporation property.
Sheba	You left the handbrake off.
Tomco	I never leave the handbrake off.

He leans on the ute shaking.

Sheba	Are you all right? Nothing happened, we escaped.
Tomco	Number three is still to come.
Sheba	From here I'm driving. You can read your submission. Aloud. Save me more of Patsy Kline.
Tomco	It doesn't want me to get there.

Scene 4: Under the mango trees, inky black shade.

Aloysius is spear-making. The others come back with armfuls of paint tubes, tubs, brushes and canvas on stretchers. Emmi goes through the stuff with Vincible. Ricky searches through a wad of unstretched paintings on the end of the wire frame bed, quite excited by what he finds.

Aloysius   That boy is lucky. Trip nearly off, but on again.

Vincible   You call that lucky or unlucky?

Aloysius   Lucky for us!

NOTES ACCOMPANYING 'FROM *ESCAPADIA*'

This play extract focuses on the interactions among six characters in an invented location called Oombulu. Sheba and Tomco are educated Indigenous cultural and social workers. Sheba, who has a sociology degree, was groomed by her matriarchal family to aim high. Tomco is older and his fluency the product of a mission education. He is regarded as an elder and high in the Law and yet works in an office in an administrative position. Neither Sheba nor Tomco talk a lot of Kriol but they are at home with Kriol. There are echoes in their spoken rhythms, tones and sometimes grammar, hence a particular style of spelling and word use. Tomco, for instance, will drop an article, and use singular words that should be plural. Syntax is regularly shortened.

''Pology fella' is what Aloysius calls Sheba whereas Vincible calls her 'honeypot'. Sheba demonstrates an anthropological interest, such as in her passion for spears, along with a sideline interest in stories, and exploration of her distant background. Aloysius makes no gender distinction in 'fella' as in the culturally generic 'im for male or female. This is part of the world the audience is shown and drawn into without explanation in the drama. Vincible's expression for Tomco as 'culture man' is a compound of considerable but not complete respect, and also a jibe. Emmi Sugarbush is a renowned artist and related to one of the old men. She is by turns indulgent and caustic with them. Ricky Duggan, an 'Indigenous Art Stimulator', is determined not to be called an arts coordinator.

Oombulu is not a word in the languages where oom and bulu are in use as syllables of other words of traditional languages, generally much longer, especially place names. It is a made-up word. The play is a fiction.

CHARACTERS

Sheba, conflict resolutionist in rapid third career incarnation
Tomco, Regional Cultural Chair, too much a solo artist and poet
Aloysius, painting senior elder, ascerbic and mercurial
Vincible, painting senior elder, ponderous but alert
Emmi, first-rank artist, elder, anthropologist's dream come true
Ricky Duggan, Community Art Stimulator

GLOSSARY
(WORDS AND EXPRESSIONS NOT EXPLAINED IN THE TEXT)

barra, short for barramundi

coolamon, an elongated carrying dish carved from wood; sometimes referred to as a ngurti

irukandji, poisonous jellyfish found in coastal seawater oceans

jaja, reciprocal grandparent–grandchild relationship; child of mother's mother

jarrampa, freshwater prawns

kartiya, non-Aboriginal person

martuwarra, river

Moke, a vehicle based on the Mini, designed by British Motor Corporation

ngapurlu, sister

pannikin, a tin cup

Puranyangu-Rangka Kerrem, a combination of Kija and Jaru words, meaning to listen, or be listened to

purluman, bullock

skin system, a sub-section group relating to a system of social organisation

swag, a bedroll or mattress and blanket

The Dry, refers to the annual dry season in Australia's tropical north

The Wet, refers to the annual wet season in Australia's tropical north

ute, an open-tray utility vehicle

willy-willy, a small, swirling gust of wind

yuwai, yes

CONTRIBUTORS

Kate Auty has degrees in Law and Environmental Science. Publications include *Black Glass: Western Australian Courts of Native Affairs 1936–1954* (Fremantle Press, 2005), and *A Jury of Whose Peers? The Cultural Politics of Juries in Australia* (coedited with Sandy Toussaint, University of Western Australia Press, 2004). Kate spent part of her childhood at the Kimberley Research Station, south of Kununurra, and one of her later years in Broome as legal adviser to Commissioner Patrick Dodson on the Royal Commission into Aboriginal Deaths in Custody. Prior to taking up her present position as the Victorian Commissioner for Environmental Sustainability, Kate worked as a magistrate in the Goldfields and Western Desert regions of Western Australia. Kate is an adjunct professor at La Trobe University's Institute for Social and Environmental Sustainability.

Peter Bibby is a broadcaster and published poet, playwright, songwriter and scriptwriter who lived for many years in Broome and worked in communities across the

Kimberley. He was awarded the Tom Collins Poetry Prize twice, and both the Donald Stuart Short Story Prize and Lyndall Hadow Short Story Prize. A former publisher with Magabala Books in Broome, and an actor in touring productions of *Bran Nue Dae* (by Jimmy Chi) and *No Prejudice* (Richard Mellick, Ningali Lawford), Peter also worked in the film industry as location manager and film fixer and was nominated for an Emmy Award by the US Academy of Motion Picture and Television Arts and Sciences in 2006.

Andrew Burke is an Australian poet with nine published books. The latest of these is *New and Selected Poems*, Walleah Press, 2012. He has lived most of his life in Perth, except for sojourns to Melbourne, Adelaide and Sydney, then – in recent years – the backblocks of China and in the Kimberley. He has also had short stories and literary criticism published. Originally influenced by jazz and blues lyrics, Andrew has written in many styles from Beat through Confessional to his style today – a mature colloquial voice often expressing narrative. Andrew has worked mainly in advertising and academia. He has an MA and a PhD from Edith Cowan University.

Jimmy Chi is a songwriter, musician and author. Born in Broome, he studied music at the Centre for Aboriginal Studies in Adelaide. His first musical play was *Bran Nue Dae*, which was widely acclaimed and performed across Australia, and has since been made into a successful film. Jimmy's second play, *Corrugation Road*, was also greeted with critical acclaim. Jimmy has been a member of the Broome-based band, Kuckles, and he co-authored (with Mick Manolis) a songbook for children titled *Broome Songwriters*.

Cathie Clement is a professional historian who has been researching and documenting Kimberley history for almost thirty years. Her efforts to preserve the region's history and heritage were recognised with the award of an OAM in 2006. Cathie's private library holds an unrivalled collection of information about the Kimberley, and she enjoys discovering 'new' items that can be added to it. Cathie has published widely about the Kimberley, and is a former president of the Perth-based Kimberley Society.

Lesley Corbett was born in Zimbabwe and immigrated to Australia in 1974, spending many years living in the Kimberley before moving to the hills outside Perth with her partner Steve Hawke and their two sons. In 1993 Fremantle Arts Centre Press published her children's picture book *Poor Fella*. A short story, 'A Change in the Weather', was published in the anthology *Summer Shorts 2* (FACP, 1994). Other published short stories are 'The Last Frontier' (*Northern Perspective* vol. 15, 1992), and 'Old Yellow' (*Northern Perspective* vol. 17, 1994).

Richard Davis is an anthropologist and poet who has worked with Indigenous and Islander groups in the Kimberley and the Torres Strait. Richard was taught to ride a horse by the Dolbys at Mt Pierre Station. He is the editor of *Woven Histories, Dancing Lives: Torres Strait Islander Identity, Culture and History* (Aboriginal Studies Press, Canberra, 2004) and, with Deborah Bird Rose, *Dislocating the Frontier: Essaying the Mystique of the Outback* (ANU E-Press, 2005). Richard lectures in Anthropology at The University of Western Australia.

Kelvin Garlett was born in a small Wheatbelt town called Kellerberrin. He is a Noongar (also sometimes spelt Nyungar) man from Western Australia's Swan River region. His father worked as a shearer for many years. Kelvin grew up on a farm; his mother raised nine children. Kelvin attended school to third-year high then left to work as a labourer in different parts of Western Australia. He learnt to shear sheep at a shearing school run by TAFE and this became his trade for the next twenty years. He met many people and learnt many things during his travels. Kelvin's hobbies are art, music, yarning around campfires, writing and reading books.

Steve Gome lived in Fitzroy Crossing in the Kimberley with his family for eighteen months in the late 1970s. It was more than twenty years later before he returned for a visit – an experience he described in an article published in *Eureka Street* in 2003. Steve is an actor, director and writer. He currently works as an Industrial Officer for the Miscellaneous Workers Union, and was recently admitted to legal practice.

Steve Hawke grew up in Melbourne but found his way to the Northern Territory and then to the Kimberley as a nineteen-year-old in 1978. Captivated by the country, the history and the people, he stayed almost fifteen years, working for Aboriginal communities and organisations. He now lives in the hills outside Perth. He continues his strong association with the Kimberley, returning most years. His writings on the Kimberley include *Noonkanbah: Whose Land, Whose Law?* (with Michael Gallagher, Fremantle Arts Centre Press, 1989), *Barefoot Kids* (FACP, 2007), a children's novel set in Broome, and the play *Jandamarra*, which premiered at the Perth International Arts Festival in 2008 and toured the Kimberley in 2011.

Leon Henry was born at Beverley in the Wheatbelt area of Western Australia. He spent his early years growing up in a family of nine children on a farm outside of Brookton where his father worked. Leon's father's side of the family is from Derby and Halls Creek, and his mother's side is from Wyndham, and also from Roebourne in the Pilbara region. His grandparents moved to the south-west of Western Australia and married into the Bennell and McGuire families. Leon has worked extensively with government in areas of community development throughout Western Australia.

C. Ann Hobson grew up in Fremantle after arriving from Manchester as a girl and now lives in Sydney. Before spending her recent years making other people's words and publications look good, she hitchhiked across the Nullarbor a few times, got chased by the Spanish Civil Guard during the first post-Franco elections, drove a mining truck, made some radio programs, wrote a few policy documents and sang in the Sydney Opera House (not all at once). Ann currently teaches media studies.

Murray Jennings is an award-winning poet and short-story writer, broadcaster and journalist, whose work has been published in magazines, newspapers and anthologies, and broadcast nationally. For over thirty years he worked in commercial and ABC radio in Western Australia and NSW and as assistant to the editor of the NSW Department of Education's *The School Magazine*. He has also worked in recording-artist promotion and for Blue Danube Radio in Vienna. Following a year as a broadcast trainer in the Kimberley, he was head of broadcasting at the Western Australian Academy of Performing Arts in Perth from 1995 to 2005. He is married, with three adult children, and now lives in Perth.

Pat Lowe has lived in the Kimberley for over thirty years. She worked as a psychologist in Broome Prison for much of that time, and has done casual and contract work for various Aboriginal organisations. She spent three years living in the desert with her partner, Aboriginal artist Jimmy Pike, with whom she collaborated on several books. Pat is a founding member of the Broome-based environmental group, Environs Kimberley. She has written a number of books for adults and children, fiction and non-fiction, about different aspects of Kimberley life, and has had stories and articles published in various magazines. She is a committee member of the small Broome publishing house, Backroom Press.

Kim Mahood is the author of *Craft for a Dry Lake*, which won several awards for non-fiction including *The Age* Book of the Year and the NSW Premier's Literary Award. She has published essays in a number of art, current affairs and literary journals. Kim is also a practising artist with work held in state, territory and regional collections. She is the only non-Indigenous artist included in the Yiwarra Kuju (Canning Stock Route) art project, and is the author of two essays in the companion publication, *Ngurra Kuju Walyja*. She lives near Canberra and spends several months each year in the Tanami and Great Sandy Deserts, working on projects with Aboriginal traditional owners. Kim's original artwork for 'Art on the run' is in colour.

Donna Bing-Ying Mak is (among other things) a mother, wife, medical practitioner and teacher. Her association with the Kimberley started in 1985 when she undertook a one-month placement at Derby Regional Hospital as a medical student. She was a community medical officer at Fitzroy Crossing from 1989 to 1993 and a regional public health physician based in Derby from 1995 to 2002. Donna has published widely on matters related to health and medicine, especially in the field of Aboriginal health. Donna would like to acknowledge Sally Blakeney for generously sharing her literary skills in 'From Hong Kong to Fitzroy Crossing'. More information about the Kimberley Medical Student Program can be found in Toussaint, S. and Mak, D., (2010) ' "If we get one back here it's worth it": evaluation of a remote area health placement program', *Rural and Remote Health* 10 (online), http://www.rrh. org.au/publishedarticles/article_print_1546.pdf

Bonita Mason is a writer, award-winning freelance journalist, and a journalism lecturer in the School of Media, Culture and Creative Arts at Curtin University. She moved to Broome from Sydney to take up a nine-month position with the Kimberley Land Council and stayed for five years. While living in Broome, she worked for Aboriginal land, media and rights organisations. She was also part of a small and active writers' group, supported the writing of others, and coedited a photographic book published by the Broome Historical Society. She returns to Broome and the Kimberley as often as she can.

Luisa Mitchell is thirteen years old and lives in Broome. She was born in Broome and has lived there all her life;

many of the Kimberley things in Luisa's story are what she has experienced. Luisa describes herself as always having her 'head in a book – soaking up stories of love, adventure, action and mystery. I love coming up with my own stories and creating different worlds in my head. I enjoy sketching, dancing, singing, reading and writing. In the future I plan to keep writing stories, reading vampire books and dancing in my living room.'

Jane Mulcock is an anthropologist who is interested in cross-cultural encounters and ideas about identity and belonging to place. Jane has undertaken research in Australia and the UK on spiritual experience, environmental beliefs and values and human–animal interactions. She is co-author of *The Salinity Crisis: Landscapes, Communities and Politics* (University of Western Australia Press, 2001) and coeditor of *Anthropologists in the Field: Cases in Participant Observation* (Columbia University Press, 2001). Jane enjoys printmaking, painting, textile arts and horse-riding.

Marminjiya Joy Nuggett is a Walmajarri woman whose family migrated from the Great Sandy Desert to the Kimberley's Fitzroy Valley in the 1960s. She lives with her husband, Gooniyandi pastoralist Jimmy Shandley, outside Fitzroy Crossing. Marminjiya has worked with organisations such as Marra Worra Worra Aboriginal Corporation. She has also worked at the Fitzroy Crossing

Hospital as a liaison officer, undertaken resource work for the Purluwarla Corporation, and contributed advice on a number of desert-related projects. 'Break a leg!' is Marminjiya's first publication.

Stephen Scourfield is an author of fiction and non-fiction. *Unaccountable Hours: Three Novellas* (UWA Publishing, 2012) is set in the landscape of Western Australia, and his novel *Other Country* (Allen & Unwin, 2007) specifically in the Kimberley; it was fiction winner in the WA Premier's Book Awards. His next novel, for publication in February 2013, is also set in the Kimberley. *Connected: A Life in Fact and Fiction* (St George Books, 2010) features the Kimberley, as do many images in his photographic book *Western Australia: An Untamed View* (St George Books, 2003). Travel Editor of *The West Australian*, he was named Australia's Best Travel Writer in both 2011 and 2009.

Pat Mamanyjun Banaga Torres is an Indigenous woman from the Torres and Drummond families of the West Kimberley. Her families are traditional owners of Jugan, Yawuru, Nyul Nyul and Jabirr Jabirr lands in the areas north and south, and around Broome. Pat has worked as an educator, writer, illustrator, manager and coordinator and is currently the Family Support Officer for the Kimberley Family Relationships Centre, Anglicare Western Australia. She also manages a small bush-tucker business called Mayi Harvests and a cultural consultancy business called Mamanyjun

Banaga Consultancy. Pat has collected her family stories for at least thirty-five years and created artworks and exhibitions both in Australia and overseas. She is a published writer and illustrator of Indigenous Australian stories that have been handed down through her own family. Her family has traditional connections to several groups in the Kimberley and her artworks are informed by traditional knowledge and images she has learned through her family.

Sandy Toussaint is an anthropologist and author who has worked in and written about the Kimberley for almost thirty years, including for the Royal Commission into Aboriginal Deaths in Custody, and the Aboriginal Land Inquiry. Her publications include *Phyllis Kaberry and Me: Anthropology, History and Aboriginal Australia* (Melbourne University Press, 1999), *Crossing Boundaries: Cultural, Legal, Historical and Practice Issues in Native Title* (edited collection, MUP, 2004) and *A Jury of Whose Peers? The Cultural Politics of Juries in Australia* (coedited with Kate Auty, University of Western Australia Press, 2004). An adjunct professor in Social and Environmental Inquiry at The University of Western Australia, Sandy has also published creative non-fiction, and a story for young children.

Robyn Wells spent her childhood in small rural Western Australian towns. She has lived in the Kimberley for over twenty-five years, producing Indigenous publications and working as an arts and literature consultant.

The current Chairperson of Backroom Press, Robyn's most recent publication is a short story in the 2010 edition of the literary journal *Indigo*.

Jacqueline Wright spent ten years as a teacher linguist working on Aboriginal language and cultural programs/projects for Western Australia's State Literature Office. As the regional literature officer, she developed literary activities and facilitated opportunities for writers in the Pilbara and Kimberley. Thanks to a Curtin University scholarship, she successfully completed a postgraduate degree in Creative Arts. This involved researching the representation of Indigenous people and knowledge by non-Indigenous writers of fiction and writing a novel drawing on her experience living and working in the remote north-west. Parts of the novel have been adapted for radio and theatre. Jacqueline is a member of Backroom Press. She currently works at Magabala Books as the Publishing Intern and at ABC Radio as Producer for Saturday Sport. Jacqueline's first novel, *Red Dirt Talking*, was recipient of the T.A.G. Hungerford Award and will be published by Fremantle Press in 2012.

ACKNOWLEDGEMENTS
SANDY TOUSSAINT

The authors and poets whose work appears in this collection have defined its qualities, and I thank each person for their experiential creativity and reflections, as well as their dedicated energy and expertise. Pat Lowe was the first person I spoke to about an idea I had for a collection of Kimberley writing as we sat drinking tea on a verandah in Broome. I have valued highly her support and incisive input ever since. Particular recognition is also due to Georgia Richter, Fremantle Press, for the collegial, perceptive and intellectually helpful way she worked with me throughout the publication process, and Ally Crimp for creative cover design. Clive Newman and Jane Fraser, Fremantle Press, believed in the collection as much as I did, and I am grateful for their encouragement. Dennis Haskell provided generous, careful guidance regarding a selection of poetry. Others who have contributed along the way include Glenice Allan, Audrey Bolger, Deborah Denton, Annette Puruta Kogolo, Bonita Mason, Ewa Nowak, Marminjiya Joy Nuggett, Aileen O'Rourke,

Lynley Tucker, and Trish Wood. Book content has also benefited from the advice of three reviewers, and I am thankful for their thoughtful feedback. The Kimberley Society and the Australia Council assisted with funding support. On a more personal level, Bree, Cade, Indi and Aidi continue to enrich my life. Their support and interest in this book, as in all other things, have been integral to bringing *Kimberley Stories* to fruition.

Andrew Burke would like to thank the White family, especially Alfie, Marcia and Yvonne, for use of the Wanalirri song in his story 'By your students you'll be taught'. He would also like to acknowledge Naomi Pigram, who sang the song on a recording made for the Catholic Education Office of Western Australia as part of a community project funded through the Commonwealth Indigenous Education Strategic Initiatives Program in 2003.